BY THE SAME AUTHOR

Prana Soup: An Indian Odyssey

Good Vibrations: A Story of a Single 60s Mum

WWOOFing North and South

The Belly Dancer

Margaret Halliday

Copyright©2018 Margaret Halliday
All rights reserved

All the characters in this book are fictitious and any resemblance to actual persons, living or dead, is purely coincidental.

ISBN-13: 978-1721662654
ISBN-10: 1721662650

To my children, Sean and Sarah
and grandchildren,
Olivia, William and Harrison

ONE

The fragrance, flavour and feel of Istanbul captivated Gemma as soon as she got off the plane. She was alone and in Istanbul for the first time; on her third night, after lying low for two days, she entered a restaurant nestled in one of the tiny alleyways off İstiklal Caddesi. She was nervous but knew this was the most famous avenue in the heart of the city and she must see it. The sound of belly dance music wafted on the warm evening air, along with the delicious smell of home-cooking, both luring her in.

'*Hoş geldiniz*, madam. Welcome to our restaurant. Would you like something to eat?' The darkly handsome waiter smiled at her, showed her to a table for two near the circular dance floor and produced a menu with a flourish and a little bow.

Gemma's heart rate quickened as she looked into the waiter's almond-shaped, deep brown eyes, the music pulsating through her, making her whole body want to gyrate to its rhythm. 'Yes, some *meze* please and a glass of white wine.'

'Certainly, madam. Local house white?'

Gemma nodded and smiled, her attention drawn to the dancer's swaying hips, her belt's golden tassels swishing to and fro as her plump belly undulated in time with the music; her breasts bounced inside a flimsy sapphire-blue bodice. Gemma had always loved to dance, even as a little girl, whirling round and round to her mother's piano playing. She had attended some belly dance classes at home in England and was told by her teacher that she showed promise. She watched every detail of the dancer's movements. *YOU could do that, she thought* – something she had never considered before.

The waiter reappeared carrying a glass of chilled white wine on a silver tray. He hovered, waiting for her to taste it. 'Hmm. That's delicious,' she said. The waiter did not go. It was early and there were few other customers. He was keen to chat.

'Are you here on holiday?' he enquired and continued to ask increasingly personal questions, which began to annoy Gemma. She became more and more distant in her replies, until he gave up, with an '*Afiyet olsun*' (enjoy your meal) and went to serve another customer who had just entered. This person was also alone, but male, so the waiter did not subject him to the same interrogation. Like Gemma, the man sat at a table for two near the dance floor and once the waiter had gone he became engrossed in the belly dancer's movements. Gemma watched him watching the dancer, intrigued by his features. He was older than her, probably in his early forties, she guessed. His face was typically Turkish: square, with a strong, straight nose, bushy black eyebrows, a thick black moustache which almost hid the upper lip of his sensuous mouth and surprisingly large, olive-green eyes. His straight, black, slightly receding hair, peppered with grey, was combed neatly back from his forehead.

When the waiter brought him a glass of *rakı*, ice and a jug of water, he pulled a packet of cigarettes from his jacket pocket. The waiter's lighter clicked. The dancer began to fix the man with her dark eyes as he sipped his *rakı* and inhaled the strong smoke of his Turkish cigarette, exhaling acrid-smelling smoke rings through his pursed lips in the direction of her nipples. She took this as a signal and went over to his table, wiggling her hips and shaking her breasts inches from his face, giving him time to stuff a one hundred lira note into her bra.

Gemma sipped her wine and nibbled her cold *meze* – stuffed vine leaves, hummus, green beans in olive oil, roasted aubergine in garlic yoghurt and artichokes, which the waiter had brought with only an '*Afiyet olsun.*' As she slowly savoured the food her fascination with the dancer's moves continued. The dancer approached her, smiling. Gemma could see she was taking in her appearance: a short-haired brunette whose fine hazel-coloured eyes were partly hidden behind thick-lensed glasses.

'You like my dance, lady?' she asked in broken English. 'Yes, very much,' Gemma said, wondering if she should also stuff her bra, but before she could do anything the dancer had reached out her hand, beckoning her onto the floor.

'Oh, no! I couldn't!' But the dancer continued to beckon, mesmerising her with her dark-eyed gaze.

The gentleman customer joined in, 'Go, go, beautiful lady!'

Gemma was warmly glowing from her second glass of wine. She stood up and let the dancer lead her to the floor. The gentleman clapped vigorously, shouting 'Bravo, bravo!'

The dancer showed surprise at Gemma's tall figure, which she could see was almost as buxom as hers, underneath an orange and yellow flowery-designed tunic top, her ensemble completed with black leggings and pumps. This was the height of fashion in England, but Gemma couldn't help but think they did little for her appearance. Nevertheless, as she began to relax to the rhythm, her movements became increasingly fluid and when more customers arrived they began to clap in time with the music, urging her on to freer and more exotic motions. The dancer, whose name she learned was Fatima, stood still, clapping with the customers as she danced and danced. Then the solo gentleman joined her on the floor, holding his arms at shoulder height, clicking his thumbs and middle fingers together as he stepped nimbly around her, despite his bulk. He was close enough for her to smell the fresh mint on his breath. *That must be strong gum he's chewing,* she thought. A boy had come in selling red roses and as they left the floor the man bought one and gave it to her. She felt embarrassed but thanked him politely.

'You dance very well,' he said, swallowing his gum.

'You're too kind. I'm not nearly as good as Fatima,' she answered, wondering how to extricate herself from the situation.

'You only need some practice, and of course the right clothes,' he said. 'I hope that I'm not bothering you but would you like to join me, as we're both alone?'

Oh dear, he's asking so politely, what can I say? I can't refuse. Gemma could have kicked herself for being so damn well-mannered. How had she got herself into this?

Her new friend introduced himself, 'My name's Mehmet and I'm the owner of this restaurant.'

She was taken aback. 'Oh, I thought you were a customer the way you were behaving with Fatima,' she blurted out, quickly adding, 'I'm Gemma, by the way.'

Mehmet produced his packet of cigarettes. 'Do you smoke?'

'No, I don't.'

'Do you mind if I do?' She minded very much but again was too polite to say.

He took a long drag of his cigarette, carefully exhaling the smoke away from her. 'I am like this with Fatima to, how do you say? Get the ball rolling?' He chuckled as he added more ice to his *rakı*.

'Oh, you mean that you encourage the other customers to do the same?'

'Exactly so. You see what is happening?' The place had filled up while they were speaking and Fatima was playing the tables, receiving many more notes stuffed into her bodice or the waist of her pantaloons.

'Yes, I do. It's a good atmosphere now.'

The waiter came with a dish of sizzling *sigara börek*: deep fried pastries stuffed with goat's cheese, in the shape of cigars. 'Please may I offer you some of these. They are our speciality – delicious.' As Gemma munched on one he continued, 'If you like, I can ask Fatima to give you some lessons and help you to buy an outfit. Then you could perform here with her.'

She nearly choked on her *börek*. 'That's an incredible idea, Mehmet, but I'm not sure if I'll have time. I'm planning to find a job teaching English and most schools have weekend lessons.'

'That's OK. You'll get a couple of days off in the week and you could perform here mid-week at first. We're quite busy then with tourists.' He beckoned to Fatima who came over, a friendly smile on her scarlet lips. She readily agreed to give Gemma lessons and gave her a business card.

'Please phone me,' she said and danced away.

Gemma studied the card. *Fatima: traditional Turkish Belly Dancing Queen*, she read. She'd come to Istanbul to be an English teacher but within one evening appeared to have embarked on another far more exciting career. How on earth had that happened?

*

Gemma had little time to think about belly dancing over the next weeks. From her hostel room she could see the massive dome and four elegant minarets of the Hagia Sophia but she was too busy searching for work as a teacher to have time to explore properly. She decided she felt more at home on the Asian side of the city rather than the European and enjoyed taking the ferry over the Bosphorus to search the myriad of streets for a permanent home.

It was a fine, if blustery, morning when Gemma hurried downhill from her hostel to the ferries. She knew that there were around eight million people living in Istanbul and it seemed that most of them were queueing for the ferries that day. The ferry landing terminals were spread out along the waterfront and she made her way to the

Kadıköy terminus, which was quiet as a ferry had just departed. She bought a token, or *jeton* from the kiosk, went through the turnstile and sat on a vacant bench, savouring a few peaceful moments before the arrival of more passengers. During the work rush it was pandemonium with hundreds of people surging onto the boats, some stumbling across the rickety gangplanks that were hastily positioned by the crew, while others simply jumped aboard, expertly judging the gap as the boat lunged to and fro in the sea. Gemma had been warned that occasionally some luckless soul misjudged the gap and fell, to be squashed to death against the ferry's side, so she gripped the rail as she stepped onto the plank and found a seat outside, downstairs, near to where she would disembark. Once the last passengers had frantically squeezed themselves on board the ferry began to cross the water. Men appeared carrying trays laden with tulip-shaped glasses of tea, saucers on top. One of them deftly handed a glass to Gemma who took it with a smile. 'May I pay?' she asked, but the seller waved her away: 'later' he said. Then came the *simit* sellers, the delicious circular, sesame-encrusted breads piled high on trays upon their heads, or held aloft on long sticks. Gemma had learned to love this snack in the short time she had been there.

She sipped her tea, breathing in the tangy sea air, the strong breeze having blown away a lot of pollution. Gulls swooped to catch pieces of *simit* thrown by upstairs passengers. The birds' urgent cries mingled with the boat engine's noise, while spray splattered the deck. Shags stood on a long sea wall, preening, wings outstretched, while more gulls soared above them, screeching and fighting for food. The magnificent Haydarpaşa railway station loomed into view and the ferry stopped, many passengers alighting to board trains bound for Istanbul's sprawling suburbs and beyond.

Minutes later the ferry docked at Kadıköy's terminus and Gemma followed the throngs out to the crowded street. She had an interview at a language school situated near the busy bazaar, on the main thoroughfare, easy to find with its large advertising billboard. The manager greeted her warmly, examined her teaching certificate, ordered *çay*, and within minutes had offered her not only a job but accommodation in one of the teachers' flats. She could hardly believe her luck. Life didn't work out so conveniently, surely?

TWO

That same day Fatima sat on another ferry boat, bound for Üsküdar, further along the coast from Kadıköy. She also watched the gulls, but often closed her eyes, losing her thoughts as the boat forged through the waves. Her reverie was suddenly disturbed by the cries of a tissue seller. Her eyes opened wide to see a packet of tissues, held almost under her nose. Startled, she looked up into her own face: the same dark eyes, the same straight nose, the same sweet lips. But the lips lacked lipstick and the girl's hair was covered in a plain bottle-green headscarf. '*Maşallah*! Who are you?' Fatima whispered, gazing in wonder at the tissue seller, who was gazing back at her, an identical expression on her face.

'Who are you, *abla*?' the girl replied.

'*Abla*? I'm not your sister, am I?' Fatima stuttered.

'Only Allah knows. I am an orphan,' the girl explained with a shrug, her eyes now downcast.

Fatima found a note in her pocket and held it out. The girl handed her the tissues, along with some change. 'No, keep the change,' she urged, thrusting the coins into the girl's hand.

'*Teşekkür ederim, abla*,' she muttered, and made to move on.

'Wait!' Fatima rummaged in her bag for her card. 'Take this.' The girl slipped it into her pocket and walked away without a backward glance.

Fatima watched the tissue seller disappear feeling numb with shock. *Who was that girl? Could it be her twin?* She was also an orphan and longed for her own family, who she could hardly remember. She had been alone for so long and had a strong sense the girl felt the same. The ferry arrived in Üsküdar and she began to walk up a steep street, flanked by old wooden houses which were sandwiched in between more modern apartment blocks. The way led to the tomb of the Sufi saint, Aziz Mahmud Hudai Efendi, whom she regularly visited. She reached the entrance, above which was written:

'O heart, if you want to taste the Divine taste

and grasp its *mahiyya*,
know that whoever enters through the gate of
Hudai will surely receive his portion.'

Fatima loved to come here. She often read the inscription over and over and particularly enjoyed the idea of grasping the divine's *mahiyya* – its very essence, its 'what-it-is-ness'. She ascended the steep steps up to the tomb, her hair now covered with a scarf and edged her way inside, where others were standing silently, palms outstretched, eyes closed. A ginger cat lay curled up in a sunlit corner, fast asleep. The devotees slowly moved around the tomb until they were close enough to lay their foreheads upon it. Fatima was filled with a vast peace, a stillness in which there were no thoughts and she stood for a while, transfixed.

All too soon, however, it was time to leave and she hastened downhill to the ferry, still wrapped in a cocoon of peace, not thinking about the coming evening and her belly dance performance. On the ferry to Karaköy she watched for the tissue seller, even though she was on a different vessel bound for the other side of the Galata Bridge from Eminönü. The girl's image seemed embedded within her cocoon, even as she hurried off the boat, past the quay's fish sellers, their cries mingling with those of the gulls, towards the Tünel, an underground funicular, which was the quickest way to the restaurant. She bought a *jeton* and sat down for the short, steep uphill ride. Now her cocoon was disintegrating as she began to focus on her evening's work.

*

Fatima hurried along the street which was crowded with early evening shoppers, tourists and people who had just finished work. It was Friday, with a weekend feel in the air, and bars and restaurants were already busy. There was an autumnal wind blowing in from the sea and a few young students sat outside cafés, huddled up in thick coats and scarves, smoking and lingering over cups of coffee. Sweet-smelling smoke from sellers of roast chestnuts assailed Fatima's nostrils and she stopped to buy a piping hot, newspaper-wrapped packet. The muezzins' call to prayer from the mosques' minarets' loudspeakers called the faithful to their Friday worship, the haunting cries mingling together as one.

Soon she reached the restaurant and hurried inside. It was already half-full and the noise of chatting customers scraping their cutlery over plates of kebabs, sipping beer, wine or *rakı*, made her feel uneasy. She loved to dance, to move to the music's rhythm, but she abhorred the furtive fumblings of drunken, leering men as they stuffed notes down her cleavage, breathing smoky alcoholic fumes into her face. She briefly wondered if the English girl – what was her name? Yes, Gemma – would contact her. It had been several weeks since her visit and she expected that she'd forgotten about her wish to learn belly dancing. She made her way through to the rear where there was a small room behind the bar. This was her dressing room and her various outfits hung on hangers behind a curtain. As she swished it open there was a knock on the door and Mehmet entered.

'Good evening, Fatima. How are you tonight?'

Fatima noticed that he was wearing a new suit, elegantly grey, with a crisply clean white shirt. He smelled strongly of recently applied cologne. 'I'm well, thank you, Mehmet Bey,' she replied politely, wondering what sort of mood her boss was in.

'Good. I'd like you to wear your turquoise outfit this evening, Fatima. Also, please include all your extra special moves. I'm expecting some important guests and they'll need five-star treatment. You'll know who they are – they'll all be male and I will put them at a table directly in front of the dance floor.'

'Of course, sir. May I ask who they are?'

Mehmet tutted, at the same time raising his bushy eyebrows ever so slightly, a subtle way of saying, 'No.' She lowered her eyes; she knew better than to annoy him. 'Right. I'll leave you to get changed,' he said, quietly closing the door behind him.

Once he was gone she dressed in her turquoise costume, which had an embroidered, sequined bodice with an exceptionally low cleavage. Around her waist was a V-shaped belt with a beaded fringe, a long, split-sided skirt beneath it. She applied her make-up with extra care, lengthening her eyelashes with thick, black mascara, her eyelids a dusky brown and her lips the colour of red rose petals. She waited patiently for the signal, a double knock on the door, and then swayed onto the dance floor, her hips moving to the rhythm of the music, her hands coiling around her shoulders like serpents. Her gaze swept the crowded restaurant, then settled on the group of five males at the front. They looked as if they had been cloned (apart from a younger one) each clad in a smart, black suit with a black tie and dark grey shirt, all sporting thin, black moustaches, their black hair slicked back with oil. They lounged lazily, their legs crossed over, deeply drawing on their cigarettes, or sipping their iced *rakıs*. Fatima did not like the look of them but nevertheless she put a sexy smile on her face and began to dance, slowly at first, her undulating movements flowing smoothly together as her belly rippled and her hips tilted. Her wavy, black hair, which reached her breasts, hung provocatively over one shoulder, to be expertly flicked over the other, followed by a shake of both of them. She began to click her finger cymbals in time with the music's beat and the crowd responded by clapping and clicking in unison. She floated across the floor, right in front of the men, gradually sank down and performed incredible contortions and leg splits, her diaphanous, turquoise veil whirling and twirling through the air. She stood up and began playing to the tables, receiving the notes and fumblings with an entrancing smile, a fluttering of her eyelashes and a *teşekkür ederim*. When she came to the VIPs' table she made a special effort. Their high denomination notes were freshly minted, their manicured hands smooth, their offerings assured and confident. She felt a shiver of fear passing through her with each proffered note, accompanied by a strong smell of expensive after-shave. The youthful one simply stared in fascination; Fatima felt unnerved by his attention and wondered about his relationship to the group.

The men stayed long after the restaurant had emptied, in deep conversation with Mehmet. Fatima rested in her dressing room, still wearing her costume as her boss had ordered her to keep it on. She nibbled at a plate of *meze* and sipped sour cherry juice, glad to finally relax. Except that she wasn't – she couldn't get the fearful sensation induced by the men out of her system.

Eventually, Mehmet opened the door, without his customary knock. Fatima noticed that he seemed unsteady and wondered if he were drunk. 'Well, Fatima. You seem to have impressed our guests – in fact they were so impressed that they'd like you to give them a private performance when they're next in town.' He stood studying her, swaying slightly.

'*Maşallah*! I am most honoured, Mehmet Bey, but this seems an odd request. Why do they want it to be private? Are they, perhaps, wanting something extra?'

'Fatima, I'll be honest with you. These men are powerful – extremely powerful, if you know what I mean? I'm not exactly sure what they expect. All I know is that if I refuse there maybe repercussions.'

'What do you mean, "repercussions"?'

'I think you are an intelligent woman, Fatima. Please don't ask me to elaborate.'

Fatima digested his response, her fearful flutterings becoming stronger. 'Do you know when they'll next be in Istanbul?' she asked, hoping that it would be a long time.

'No, I don't, Fatima, but I need you to agree to their request. It'll be financially good for you. You'll get far more money than you earn here and I won't take my usual percentage – you may keep all their tips.'

'Mehmet Bey, I'm a belly dancer, interested only in the art of dance. I hate the way some of the customers tip me.'

'I know, I'm sorry, but you must think of it as a business, and the sexier you are, the more money you will receive. This is life, unfortunately.' He looked at his watch. 'It is very late. Let me call you a taxi and we can discuss this more when you are rested.'

Fatima felt completely exhausted but sleep did not come easily that night. She thought about her boss: he had never asked her to do anything shady before. Somehow he had got into the clutches of these powerful men and now it seemed that she was also in them. She had no-one to protect her. Should she run away? But where to? She had already done that and she did not wish to do it again. The image of the black-suited men was stamped on her mind as she struggled to rest.

THREE

'Where you from?'
'Are you married?'
'Have you children?'

Gemma rapidly realised that she would have to abandon her carefully planned first lesson with this group of elementary students. She ventured out from behind the safety of her front desk, conjured up a warm smile and simultaneously relaxed her pose. 'I'm from the south of England,' she told a curly-haired young man, who grinned back, pleased to have understood her reply. 'No, I'm not married,' she informed another friendly youth, aware that the rest of the class were pleasantly surprised by her answer, especially the young men. She quickly informed them that she had no children, which caused the girls to giggle and the boys to laugh at her suggestion of even having children when she wasn't married. When asked her age she rolled her eyes, stating the well-worn, 'You should never ask a lady her age,' which produced nods of support from the young women, who were all fashionably dressed, well made-up and headscarf-less.

She had been shocked by the barrage of personal questions and when she arrived back at her flat she told her flatmate, an amiable American in her mid-twenties called Tina, all about it. 'That's Turks for you,' she replied with a rueful smile. 'They're all most inquisitive. It's the culture so you're just gonna have to get used to it. They'll complain about you if you're unfriendly.'

'Is that right?' Gemma was horrified at the thought of getting a complaint.

'Sure. It happened to me with my first class. I ignored their questions and ploughed on with grammar exercises from the book. The next day I was summoned to the Principal's office. They'd complained and wanted another teacher. She gave me a different class and told me to answer their questions and be friendly. I did that and everything's been fine since.'

'Well, I guess I did the right thing,' Gemma said with a relieved sigh.

'Yeah, you sure did.' Tina handed her a cold bottle of Efes Pilsen. 'Here, let's chill.'

Gemma was only too keen to have a glass of cold beer after her stressful lesson and sipped contentedly, watching the street below through the bay window, which jutted out above it, allowing her to study the throngs of Saturday afternoon shoppers, laden with bags from the nearby Kadıköy bazaar.

Never having travelled further than Western Europe she was still experiencing culture shock, slowly becoming accustomed to blatant stares from passers-by, particularly men, while learning to avoid eye contact. She had also seemed to cause the clicking of tongues, which, she discovered, was a sign of disapproval at her sleeveless, low cut tops. At least now, with the approach of autumn, she needed to cover up against cooler air, wind and rain. The cries of an *eskici* floated through the window and she saw an old man pushing a cart, on which were an assortment of discarded household objects, including a rusty chain and a metal bowl. He searched the windows for heads shouting at him to come and collect unwanted items, in exchange for a few lira. From a window above a *bakkal* an ancient woman with a flowery headscarf lowered a basket down past the displays of washing powder, packets of tea, sacks of flour and sugar with her gnarled fingers. To Gemma's amusement the shop's lad appeared, took out a piece of paper, then reappeared with a long loaf of bread and a bottle of milk, which he carefully placed in the basket. Gemma tried to imagine this happening in her English village, and chuckled to herself at the absurdity of it.

She never tired of watching the constantly changing scene below, but was less keen to join in. She shared the cooking with Tina and it was her turn that evening. Reluctantly she put on her coat and grabbed her shopping bag. 'Gemma, can you take the empties out, please,' Tina asked.

'OK,' Gemma replied grumpily, as she thrust empty milk and beer bottles into a plastic bag. She did not like the judgemental look she received from the grocer as he took the beer bottles, giving her a few lira in return. Another hassle was the heavy, five-litre glass drinking water containers, which also needed to be recycled. She wished that she was an elderly lady, lowering a basket in which one of the water bottles would be deposited.

She wound her way through the crowds to the bazaar's food area, hurrying past butchers' shops outside of which were enclosed, transparent boxes, full of sheep's heads; she averted her gaze from their stares, as if they were Turkish men. Next, the pungent smell of fresh fish overpowered her; so many varieties were displayed, types that she'd never seen before, their bright red gills proving their freshness. A babble of voices filled the air: vendors shouting, '*Buyurun,*' trying to attract the crowd's attention while shoppers haggled, with raised voices, big hand gestures and much tongue clicking as they struck fierce bargains. They ignored the small boys who hovered nearby, holding out handfuls of lemons. One followed Gemma after she had bought some rocket, mint and crisp lettuce, imploring her to buy with such huge, sad brown eyes that she relented, thrusting a few coins into his grimy palm in return for the fruit. Head-scarfed women tut tutted in disapproval as they passed by because the lemons were over-priced. She had quickly learned that it was impossible to purchase one or two pieces of fruit or vegetables – the sellers simply laughed at her. Half a kilo was the minimum quantity they would sell, the prices being so low that it was easier to purchase by the kilo, although it made a heavy load to carry. Other small boys offered to help with the bags, again for a small sum, and at times, when Gemma was laden, she let them.

*

As the days passed, Gemma became used to her routine. She taught on Saturday and Sunday mornings for three hours, which ruled out a wild weekend social life. On week days she had split shifts, with morning and evening classes. Her flat was near the school so she was able to go home for a rest in the afternoons. Wednesdays and Thursdays were her days off and she relished her free time, initially relaxing at home but later she began to explore. One sunny Thursday morning she decided to take a ferry to the Princes' Islands, out in the Sea of Marmara. She got off at the first stop, Kınalıada (Henna Island), and began to walk through the small harbour town, admiring the fine, old wooden mansions and relaxing in the tranquillity of the place. There were no motorised vehicles, except service ones, only bicycles and horse-drawn carriages were allowed. As she walked along she noticed the absence of stares and other hassle and decided to venture out of the town, up a hill into the countryside. A young man wearing a navy-blue tracksuit began to walk alongside her, and such was her mood of relaxation that she responded to his friendly, 'Hello.'

'Where are you going?' he asked.

She decided to practise her Turkish, which she had been studying, but had little opportunity to use, except when she was shopping. 'I'm going for a walk, it's such a lovely day.'

'Can I accompany you?'

'Yes. I can practise my Turkish,' she laughed. As they continued walking up the hill she discovered that his father was an estate agent on the island. 'It's such a wonderful place to live,' she said. 'I might buy a house here myself. How much are they?'

The youth agreed that it was indeed a splendid place, but he seemed unwilling to discuss prices. They were some way from the town, the bare hills with a few scrubby bushes surrounding them, when he began to move nearer to her. A tiny flash of fear passed through her and she inched away. In response he moved closer again, at the same time saying, 'You are a very beautiful woman.'

Gemma laughed nervously. 'How old are you?'

'I'm eighteen,' he said.

'Well, I'm much older than you,' Gemma replied, hoping that this would dampen his ardour.

They were still walking, but at a slower pace. Then he stopped, fixed her with his eyes and said, 'Have sex, lady?'

Gemma stood still, her blood pounding from adrenaline. She was angry and scared and let loose with a tirade of English. 'What a cheek you've got, you disgusting animal! Go away! Leave me alone!'

He stood mournfully, uncomprehending, his hands in his pockets. She couldn't help noticing a bulge in his tracksuit, which increased her fury. Finally, she stopped and stood glaring at him. 'What, no sex lady?' he asked, disappointment enveloping him like a cloud.

'No!' Gemma shouted, then turned and walked as fast as she could down the hill towards the town. *Don't run*, she told herself, steeling herself not to look back, until she felt it safe to do so. He was some distance away, making for a bush on the hillside. She breathed a sigh of relief, then laughed out loud. But she was also upset at what had happened. She realised that even in this peaceful spot it was impossible to relax and to walk alone as a woman.

*

One Sunday afternoon Gemma went on an outing with some of her students after their lesson. They loved to drive along the road beside the Bosphorus, towards the Black Sea. Unfortunately, many other drivers had the same idea, so they crawled along in slowly moving traffic for most of the way. Gemma gazed out of the window at the sea, which was busy with ferry boats, fishing boats and huge cargo ships, miraculously avoiding one another. They stopped for a break at Çamlıca ferry landing stage where there was a small café. Ayhan, the car driver, proudly announced, 'You can eat the tastiest yoghurt in Istanbul here.' They managed to find an empty table and he quickly summoned the waiter and ordered small tubs of creamy yoghurt, on which they sprinkled what tasted like sherbet.

'Hmm, it's delicious,' Gemma said, then paused to look at a young woman who had approached their table, holding out a packet of tissues and asking for money. Gemma usually ignored the constant hassle from sellers of a wide variety of stuff, from nail clippers to children's toys, but this particular girl and her voice seemed familiar. Ayhan and the waiter were both doing their best to shoo the lass away, but Gemma held out her hand for the tissues, searching the girl's dark eyes which stared into hers in a strangely disturbing way.

'Why did you buy those tissues?' Ayhan asked, 'they are selling them at too high a price. You shouldn't encourage them.'

'I'm sorry, Ayhan, but she reminded me of someone.'

'Maybe she's her twin,' he said jokingly. Gemma laughed, telling herself not to be stupid.

They got back into the cars, continuing along the Bosphorus until they arrived at Anadolu Kavağı, the last ferry stop on the Asian side before the Black Sea. It was a pretty little place, with old wooden houses built right by the water which lapped at their foundations. At the ferry landing and strung out along the road beside the sea were numerous restaurants, each specialising in fresh fish and *midye tava*, fried mussels in crispy batter on a skewer, served with garlic sauce. Ayhan led the way into one of the larger establishments, which was built out over the water, giving a fine view of the Bosphorus and the hills of the European shore. They clustered around a large table at the window and all ordered the mussels, accompanied by glasses of white, frothy *ayran*, a salty, refreshing yoghurt drink. *This is definitely the way to experience Istanbul*, Gemma decided as she relaxed, letting her students' Turkish wash over her. In a group of Turks like this she was unlikely to receive any unwanted advances.

Dusk was falling as they left the restaurant, and Gemma wrapped her woollen scarf tightly around her neck against the evening chill. As they crawled back along the shore the lights of the city were reflected in the turbulent waters of the Bosphorus, which was still busy with brightly lit ships and boats. They passed underneath the Bosphorus Bridge, packed with slowly moving traffic, a toxic mix of exhaust fumes filling the air, the sounds of their engines a distant hum. When they reached Kadıköy Ayhan asked, 'Can I drop you here in the main street?'

'Yes, of course,' Gemma replied, aware of the difficulty of driving through the narrow streets surrounding the bazaar. She hurried homewards, skillfully avoiding eye contact as she negotiated the still crowded pavements.

Tina was attempting to understand a Turkish sitcom on TV when Gemma arrived at the flat. 'So, how was your trip?' she asked.

'Really good, except for the traffic jams.'

'Yeah, I told you things would be OK if you were friendly with your students.'

'Yes, they're such nice people and they wouldn't allow me to pay for anything.'

'No, in fact you hurt their pride if you offer to pay.'

'Oh dear! Have I committed another faux pas?'

'Don't worry – they're getting used to the ways of foreigners,' Tina said reassuringly.

That night Gemma dreamed that she was running through traffic on the Bosphorus Bridge, when suddenly, frantically flapping her arms, she became airborne, soaring high into the blue sky, while people stuck in their cars far below gazed upwards, shielding their eyes from the sun's glare, watching open-mouthed as she flew higher and higher, away over the forests bordering the Black Sea.

She snapped awake. Fatima! That was who the tissue seller looked like. Those eyes! It hadn't been the glamorous, talented Fatima of course, but how similar they were. The tissue seller had the same dark eyes except hers were so much more haunted. Where was that card with Fatima's details? She must find it. She had a strong urge to see her again. She lay awake awhile, listening to the faint boom of the ships' foghorns as they waited their turn to sail up the Bosphorus Strait, finally falling into a troubled sleep.

FOUR

Gemma was still thinking about Fatima when she awoke to the sound of rain smashing into her bedroom window, accompanied by a wind which she imagined was tugging the remaining leaves from the plane trees in her back yard. She snuggled down under the duvet, not wanting to get up and face the wild weather. *Just another five minutes.* An hour later she woke with a start. *Oh, no, she was going to be late for class.* In a panic she scrambled into her clothes, gulped down a cup of instant coffee, threw on her waterproof coat and rushed out into the crowds. She hurried along, ducking to avoid umbrellas while trying not to step into deep puddles. Istanbul in the rain was a vile, dirty place and Gemma had quickly realised it was impossible to completely remove the muddy stains from her clothes.

It wasn't until the end of her morning lessons, as she was going home for lunch through the rain-sodden streets, that she remembered Fatima's card. The rain had stopped and a pale sun shone through milky clouds, allowing Gemma to slow her pace as she observed a small group of street cats. They were fighting over some fish scraps, spitting and yowling at each other. She paused to buy a bunch of yellow chrysanthemums from a dark-skinned woman sitting on a stool in a small square, surrounded by buckets of autumnal flowers. The smell of freshly baked bread enticed her into a bakery for a long, white loaf.

There was no sign of Tina when she reached their flat. She guessed that she'd gone out for lunch and prepared herself a sandwich. Then she began to search for Fatima's card and found it at the bottom of a pile of papers. She tried phoning her home number, but there was no reply and no answer machine. She kept trying, feeling a mixture of apprehension and excitement at the prospect of belly dancing in front of an audience. Finally, the following Saturday afternoon, Fatima answered her call and in Gemma's best Turkish they arranged to meet at the restaurant the following Wednesday around mid-day.

*

Wednesday morning dawned bright and sunny, although as Gemma boarded the Karaköy ferry a chill wind forced her to turn up the collar of her jacket. People were sitting outside, well wrapped up against the cold, some eating sunflower seeds, spitting their shells surreptitiously into their hands, before shaking them over the rail into the sea. Others, mainly men, were smoking, inhaling deeply then chucking the tips into the water. Gemma shook her head in disgust. How could they treat this beautiful city like that? As the boat gathered speed across the choppy strait, it bounced through the waves, throwing spray up onto the deck, forcing Gemma and the other outside passengers to draw their legs in hastily to avoid getting wet. It was not rough enough to go inside so Gemma sat, enjoying the boat's rhythm, the salty spray brushing her face, the wheeling gulls crying high above.

    She negotiated the wooden gangplank, which wobbled as the sea churned beneath the boat, then quickly joined the crowds moving towards the Tünel, avoiding eye contact with swarthy-looking men selling packets of condoms. The red light district was further up the hill near the Galata Tower which Gemma had visited, marvelling at the views of the Bosphorus, the Golden Horn, the Topkapı Palace, the great mosques and other sights from its circular restaurant. By contrast, prostitutes were kept hidden behind high gated walls in the nearby Beyoğlu area; Gemma never ventured there having heard about its dangers.

    She emerged from the Tünel into İstiklal Caddesi, where mainly tourists were boarding the two-coach red wooden tram which ran along the pedestrianised street to Taksim Square. She passed by it, along with the noisy crowds and paused to admire beautiful, polished wooden saz, or Turkish lutes, hanging in a music shop's window. People were buying roasted corn-on-the-cobs, the discarded remains of which were pecked at by flocks of pigeons. Gemma was trying hard to locate the side alley where the restaurant was. She knew it was at the Taksim Square end of the avenue and finally found it, half-hidden between a kebab shop, the smell of grilled meat hanging in the air, and a newsagent. She spotted the sign, *Belly Dance Every Evening*, and pushed open the door.

Fatima came to greet her, kissing her on both cheeks, which surprised Gemma after only one meeting. 'Welcome to our restaurant again, Gemma,' she said, a genuine-looking smile on her face.

It was still early for lunch and Gemma looked around at empty tables. Fatima asked her if she was hungry but she only needed water so she took her backstage and poured her a cool glassful. Gemma relished the liquid slipping down her parched throat.

'So, would you like to dance here?' Fatima asked, fixing Gemma with an appraising look.

Gemma gave a nervous laugh and shifted her eyes from Fatima's. 'Maybe, but I'm not sure I will ever be good enough.'

'You will be once I've shown you some more moves and you've had a chance to practise,' Fatima assured her.

'You're very kind.'

'No, I'm not being kind. I'm telling the truth. You've got the basic moves, like the Figure Eight.'

Gemma interrupted, 'What do you mean by "Figure Eight"?'

'I'll show you.' Fatima put on a belly dance music tape, stood up and moved her right hip forward, away from her body, back, then back to the centre. Her left hip moved back, into the centre, forward and then away from her body.

'Yes, I understand now,' said Gemma, standing up and joining in the movement.

'That's good,' said Fatima approvingly, 'but lift your hips higher, like this.'

Gemma followed her lead, happy to be dancing again. 'Very good, bravo!' Fatima laughed. 'Now I'll show you some arm and head movements.' Gemma watched as she raised her hands above her head, palms together with her shoulders down. There was a full-length mirror on the wall and Fatima told Gemma to check her posture as she went into the position. They were just practising some head movements when there was a soft knock on the door. 'Come in,' Fatima said.

'Oh! Pardon,' Mehmet Bey said, as he peered round the door.

'It's OK, come in, come in,' Fatima said encouragingly.

'I'm sorry to disturb you, but I heard the music and wondered what was happening as you're not usually here now.' He stood, taking in the scene, abstractedly rubbing his moustache with his left hand, on which flashed a ruby ring.

'I'm teaching Gemma some dance moves,' Fatima explained.

'*Hoş geldiniz*, Gemma,' he said politely, extending his right hand, which was slightly sweaty.

'*Hoş bulduk*,' she replied.

'Ah! You have been learning some Turkish,' he said, and continued with the Turkish greetings, which Gemma responded to completely correctly. 'Bravo, Gemma. So now Fatima is going to teach you how to belly dance. Would you like to perform here after that?'

'Maybe, Mehmet Bey, but I'll have to be much better than I am now.'

'Nonsense! You only need to learn some different moves and you'll be fine. Of course, you'll also need to buy an outfit, unless Fatima is willing to lend you something.'

'That's not a problem.' Fatima gestured towards her wardrobe. 'I have a lot of outfits and we are about the same size.'

Gemma gazed at the beautiful rainbow of colours, glittering in the corner of the room. Could it be true that she would dance in public wearing such revealing, tantalising things?

FIVE

Fatima was delighted with Gemma whose dancing got better and better as she attended every Wednesday for lessons. She had mastered complicated floor movements and arm positions, which she had practised for hours at home. When she first tried on one of her costumes, a frilly, hip-hugging, scarlet full-length skirt with a beaded waist and matching sequined bodice, Fatima gasped in amazement. 'Gemma, you are so beautiful.' The outfit had transformed her friend, as she now regarded Gemma, into a completely different person. The only problem was her glasses. How could she tactfully broach this subject?

Gemma made it easy for her. 'I know what you're thinking, Fatima. My glasses!' She took them off and squinted around the room.

'Well, could you manage without them?'

'I can try. If not, maybe I can get some contact lenses.'

'That's a good idea – you look so much better with no glasses.'

They had been having snacks at the restaurant, but one day after a practice session Gemma asked about the nearby *pide salonu*. Fatima explained it was a café specialising in *pide*, a Turkish pizza, made with cheese or minced meat, tomatoes and onions. 'Shall we go now?' she suggested thinking how good it would be to get out of the restaurant. As they sat eating and chatting at a corner table with a view of the busy street, Fatima felt herself relax. She realised how much strain she'd been under since her encounter with the black-suited men. Every day she'd been on the lookout for them. They hadn't returned yet but she felt it was only a matter of time and that thought kept her nerves on edge.

So far her conversations with Gemma had focussed mainly on the dance moves and her new friend's life in Istanbul. Despite Gemma's rapidly improving Turkish there was still a language barrier, with constant references to a Turkish-English dictionary, which slowed communication and restricted them to simple subjects. This first meal, outside the confines of the restaurant, however, seemed to have an effect on both of them, so that when Gemma asked her about her early life, she felt able to reveal a little.

'I was born in Eastern Turkey, not far from the border with Iraq and my first language is Kurdish,' she began.

'What was that like?' Gemma asked, leaning forward and listening closely, trying to make sense of Fatima's slow but complex Turkish.

'We lived in a tiny mountain village, clinging to a remote, bare hillside. It was buffeted by winter's blizzards and baked in the fierce summer sun.'

'Please speak very slowly and give me time to look up these new words,' Gemma begged.

Fatima smiled patiently at her, taking a sip of water and quietly recollecting her childhood.

'We have something in common – I was also born in a village, but it was in the flat, green English countryside, without harsh weather conditions, just soft rain and weak sunshine.'

'Yes, very different and I think that you were not living in poverty like we were.'

'That's true. My family weren't rich but they weren't poor either. My father's a civil servant and my mum's a teacher.'

'Ah, so you have the same job as your mother.'

'Well, sort of. She's a primary school teacher, that's children from five to eleven, but I teach adults. Anyway, enough about me. Please tell me more, Fatima.'

Fatima sat silently for a moment, lost in thought, trying to decide what to say and wondering if she should say anything. But she began, hesitantly, fiddling with a lock of her hair, twisting it round her fingers, then straightening it out. 'We were a large family. I have three older brothers and two big sisters.'

'So you're the baby?' Gemma said, smiling encouragingly.

'Yes. There were no more children after me.' Fatima paused, then took a deep breath, as if to dive down deep. 'My mother died in childbirth,' she finally said, then stopped.

Gemma reached for her hand, the one not twisting her hair, and squeezed it. 'Oh, Fatima! I am so sorry,' she cried, shocked at her friend's ashen face.

Fatima thought, but did not say, *and what about the other? The one that finally killed her?* A tear ran down her face and she quickly brushed it away.

Please stop, Fatima, if you are too upset.' Gemma said, withdrawing her hand.

'No, no. It's OK. What else do you want to know?'

'Well, if you're sure? What happened after that? Were you brought up by your father?'

'No. My father was a shepherd. He was always on the mountainsides herding his flocks of sheep and goats with his fierce Turkish sheepdog. We called his dog *Aslan*, because he was like a ferocious golden lion, although with us children he was as soft as a lamb. My dad became very depressed after Mum died and I was given to my aunt, his youngest sister, to be looked after. She was already feeding my baby cousin, so she fed me too.'

'That was kind of her, wasn't it?'

'Turkish families are very close, especially in the east, so it was normal.'

'What became of your brothers and sisters?'

'My oldest brother and sister were in their teens, so they took over the running of the household. Children have to grow up fast in these poor places. They either leave school early or they don't go at all, especially the girls.'

'That's terrible. Did you go to school?'

'Actually, I did. My aunt was quite intelligent and modern and she insisted on all her children, including me, attending the local school.'

'So, that was good, wasn't it?'

'Yes, it was. But . . .'

'But what?' Gemma pressed, dying to hear the rest of the sentence. But the words hung in the air.

'I'm so sorry, Gemma, but I must stop there. It's too upsetting for me.'

'Oh, Fatima, certainly you may stop if you need to.'

Fatima wiped away another tear. *How can I tell my dear friend what happened to me? I want to, I really want to; I've never told anyone and it sits like a boulder inside me.* She looked at her watch, gave herself a little shake and gave Gemma a watery smile. 'I have to go now, Gemma. It's getting late and I need to prepare for this evening's work.'

'Of course. I'll chum you to the restaurant,' Gemma said, summoning the waiter and paying the bill. Fatima tried to protest.

'You've given me so much of your time, Fatima,' she insisted.

'For you, dear Gemma, my time is free.' She looked at her friend's happy face and momentarily forgot her troublesome past.

As they walked along the street Gemma asked, 'When do you think I'll be ready to start dancing for real?'

'For real? You mean in the restaurant?' Gemma nodded.

'Well, I think you could begin next week,' she said.

'You really think I'm ready?'

Fatima gazed into Gemma's sparkling eyes. *Was she right to encourage this sweet, naïve English girl?* The image of the oddly menacing-looking men returned again, causing her to shiver. She pulled her woollen shawl tighter around her shoulders.

'Yes, indeed you are,' she said, trying to sound confident.

'Well, if you're sure . . . .' Gemma said, then added, 'I'll need to buy an outfit. Would you help me?'

'Remember I said that you may wear one of mine. That scarlet skirt and bodice, for instance. You looked so good in that costume.'

'Oh, that's too kind of you.'

'You might not like it, so there's no point in buying yourself one yet.'

'What do you mean, I might not like it?'

Fatima stopped walking, causing the crowds to move around them impatiently, with a few mutterings. 'I mean, the drunks stuffing money down your bodice, in your waistband, groping you, leering at you, breathing their foul alcohol laden breath in your face and blowing smoke rings at you.'

Gemma stood, trying to make sense of this stream of Turkish. 'I think I understand what you are saying but I don't think they'll do this to me – I'm not as sexy as you, Fatima.'

'Not as sexy as me! Of course you are! And being English means that they'll find you even more attractive.'

'Well, I'll try it out next week and then we'll see,' Gemma said.

They had resumed walking and were at the entrance to the restaurant's street. 'Let's say "goodbye" here,' Fatima said and gave Gemma a hug. 'Come around five next Wednesday and I'll make up your face.' She gave Gemma a worried look.

'Don't look so anxious, it'll be fine,' Gemma smiled and as she did so Fatima imagined that pretty face made up with alluring eyeliner and ruby-red lipstick. Fatima attempted to smile back but she did not feel reassured.

SIX

Whenever Gemma thought about her first belly dance performance she felt a mixture of excitement and nervousness. *What if she forgot some moves or, worst of all, fell to the floor, instead of gliding gracefully down?* She tried to concentrate on her teaching, pushing her doubts away.

Tina was beginning to get into a festive mood. 'It'll be Christmas soon,' she greeted Gemma on Friday evening, as they drank beers at home after a hard day's work.

'That's going to be a non-starter,' Gemma said miserably.

'I know they don't celebrate it here but we can,' Tina insisted. 'We've got Christmas Day off, so that's something.'

'Yes, but the Turks don't get that off.'

'I know, but surely we can find other Christians to celebrate with?'

'I don't even know if I am Christian,' Gemma said.

'So, what are you then?' Tina glared at her.

'Why are you getting so uptight? I didn't think you were religious?'

'Well, I'm not, except at Christmas. And Easter. For the eggs.' Tina took a glug of beer and her expression changed from aggressive to appeasing.

Gemma laughed. 'So, you're just a party Christian, aren't you?'

'OK, I guess, but we should do something.'

'Hmm. Christmas is on a Friday, so we'll get three days off. We could go somewhere. Get out of this stinking city and breath some fresh air,' Gemma said, picturing a magical place, full of greenery and pollution free.

'Now that's an idea! I've got a permanent cough from the foul air – it's all that coal they burn in the winter. There's supposed to be gas coming in soon which should improve the air quality.' Tina coughed on cue.

'There's still all the traffic fumes though. It's great on the islands with hardly any cars,' Gemma said, dreamily.

'As long as you don't chat to any guys,' Tina remarked, her face splitting into a mischievous grin.

'Ugh! Don't remind me,' Gemma shuddered.

Tina was silent for a moment, then she cried, 'I've got it! One of my students told me about a great place – it's a *termal*, where there are hot springs and forests.'

Gemma sat up expectantly. 'It sounds wonderful. Where is it?'

'It's in the hills near Yalova.'

'Yalova? Isn't that a way over the Sea of Marmara?'

'Yes, but you can get a ferry or even a sea bus, which is super-fast.' Tina was becoming increasingly excited.

Gemma was less positive. 'Where does the sea bus go from and how do we get there? And is there anywhere we can stay?'

'Whoa! Too many questions, Gemma. I'll be seeing the student who told me about it tomorrow and I'll get more details from him.'

'OK, you do that and then we'll decide.'

*

After their Saturday classes Gemma and Tina went to a restaurant near the school with some of their students. The place was full, mainly with men, all speaking loudly as they smoked, drank *rakı* or beer and ate *meze* and kebabs. Hasan, an older student, managed to find a free table and they all crowded around it, ignoring the men's stares. 'Don't worry about those old guys,' Hasan said, as he beckoned to one of the busy waiters.

Ruhane, a pretty girl with long, curly black hair and a flawless complexion, added, 'Hasan's right. Our country is full of ignorant men who stare at women and harass them.' The other female students nodded vigorously in agreement, while the males tried to look intelligent and serious.

Once their drinks had arrived Tina turned to Gemma and said, 'Hasan knows all about the *Termal*, don't you, Hasan?'

'Yes. I have been there several times with friends or family. It's a lovely place with clean air and forests.'

'How do you get there?' Gemma asked.

'From Kadıköy the quickest way is to get the commuter train from Haydarpaşa station to Kartal. From there you can get a sea bus or a ferry to Yalova. It takes about two hours all together.'

Gemma frowned. 'It sounds like quite a trek.'

'Yes, I suppose it is, but it's worth it. Within Istanbul itself, travel can take as long as that. At least you won't be stuck in a traffic jam,' Hasan said.

'OK, I guess it could be quite enjoyable, especially the sea bus part. Where can we stay when we arrive there?'

'There's a posh hotel actually at the *Termal*, or you may stay in a *pansiyon*, or guest house, in the village of Gökçedere nearby.'

'That's more for us, isn't it Tina?'

'It sure is, the amount of money we earn,' Tina laughed.

'I think you earn more than we do,' Hasan remarked, causing the teachers some embarrassment. Tina rapidly changed the subject and asked the students what they would be doing for New Year.

'We'll have a big party with our friends and family,' said Ruhane.

'What will you both do?' Hasan asked.

Tina looked at Gemma, who shrugged. 'We'll get Christmas out the way first,' said Gemma, thinking, *and my belly dance performance.*

*

Before Gemma knew it, it was Wednesday morning. She awoke with a start, coming out of a strange dream where she was running and running along never ending dark alleyways, pursued by something sinister. She lay staring at a cobweb in the corner of the ceiling, trying to escape the dream's clutches. *Well, tonight's the night*, she thought, feeling strangely calm after her last few days of nervousness. She showered meticulously, rubbing and scrubbing with her favourite lemon-scented soap.

'Wow, you smell nice,' Tina greeted her as she sat down at their kitchen table.

'Thanks, and so does this kitchen. Is there enough coffee for me?'

'Sure. Help yourself. I thought I'd treat us to some fresh stuff today,' Tina said, taking a mouthful of the pungent brew. She looked closely at Gemma. 'So, how do you feel about tonight?'

Gemma ran her fingers through her damp hair. 'It's funny. I've been so on edge but now it's nearly here I feel really chilled.'

'That's great! But you'll need a bit of an adrenaline rush this evening.'

'I'm sure that'll happen, Tina,' said Gemma, pursing her lips and lifting her eyebrows.

'I can come with you, if you want.'

'No! That'll make me too nervous.'

'I can't see why. I'd have thought it would help to have a friendly face in the audience.'

'I'm sorry, Tina. I can't explain. I just know that I need to do this by myself. Fatima'll be there – she'll give me support.'

'OK. Well, if you're sure. . .'

'Sure I'm sure. I'll let you come and see me when I'm world famous.'

'Yeah, right. Not any time soon then.' Tina washed down a slice of toast with the rest of her coffee and got up. 'I'm off out to do some shopping so I guess I won't see you until later.'

'Don't wait up for me. I could be really late.'

'Try not to be, or I'll worry about you.'

'That's sweet, but you're not my mum.'

'OK. Point taken, but be careful.' With that advice she threw on her coat and headed for the door.

Gemma slowly sipped her coffee and munched toast. Tina had a point – she must be careful. She would leave early if possible to catch the last ferry from Karaköy. The day stretched ahead, a steady drizzle leaking out of the sky. She decided to immerse herself in work for the remainder of the morning in order to banish all negative thoughts about the coming night.

By lunchtime the drizzle had eased and a watery sun was attempting to shine through a sodden sky. Gemma walked briskly along the street in the direction of Moda, a more fashionable part of town than Kadıköy, situated on a point of land where the Bosphorus meets the Sea of Marmara. The air was fresher there with an open aspect across the boat-studded water to the Topkapı Palace and the Blue Mosque, the Hagia Sophia completing the marvellous view.

Gemma found a small café overlooking this scene and ordered a bowl of *mercimek çorbası*, which came with chunks of fresh lemon and a plate piled high with crusty white bread. She adored this soup, almost like the lentil soup her mother made at home. It was her comfort food and she followed it with rice pudding: '*Sütlaç*, please,' she told the waiter. She took a first mouthful of the delicious cinnamon dessert, savouring the caramelised skin. She smiled to herself, pleased with her improving Turkish. She was really beginning to feel at home here. Afterwards she wandered further along and drank *çay* at one of the open-air cafés. As she gazed across the sea, watching the cargo ships cruising up the strait, she pictured herself dancing on their decks, her scarlet skirt twirling in the breeze.

The time, which had seemed to be sliding slowly by, suddenly speeded up, causing Gemma to start when she looked at her watch. *I'd better get going if I want to be there by five.* She hurriedly paid her bill. She arrived at the ferry terminal to see the doors slid shut, the last few passengers dashing across the gangplanks as the boat's horn sounded and it began to turn towards Karaköy, churning up the sea. She paced, waiting for the next ferry, watching the minutes tick by, hurrying on board when it did arrive. She sat outside, breathing in the sea air deeply, feeling herself relax and her mind become still. Then the boat bumped into the rubber tyres tied to the sides of the landing stage and she was once again rushing off it, past the fish sellers towards the Tünel, where she just missed a train. She hastened through the late afternoon crowds on İstiklal Caddesi, finally reaching the restaurant ten minutes late which Gemma considered 'on time' in Istanbul.

*

Fatima was sitting at a window table, the only sign of life in the deserted restaurant. She jumped up when she saw Gemma, planting a kiss on both her cheeks. 'It's so good to see you,' she exclaimed. 'I wondered if you'd come.'

'I was wondering that myself the last few days, but now I feel much calmer.'

'Good. Let's go to my room and I'll make up your face and do something to your hair,' Fatima said, giving her friend's hair a critical look.

'My hair's very difficult to keep tidy. It's so thick and wavy and does its own thing.'

'Don't worry. I'll sort it out,' Fatima said soothingly. With that she went to work, dampening Gemma's unruly locks then blow drying them into shape.

Gemma regarded herself in the mirror. 'That's amazing Fatima!

How did you do that? I don't have the patience to fiddle around with my hair.'

'You just need some practice. Anyway, I'm not finished yet, there's still your face to do.' She deftly applied a light foundation to Gemma's skin. 'Your skin's so good it doesn't need much make-up,' she observed. Next she rubbed brown eyeshadow onto Gemma's eyelids, then black eyeliner and thick, dark brown mascara. Finally, she coloured her lips with a bright red lipstick. She stood back, surveying her handiwork. 'Well, what do you think?' she asked.

Gemma peered into the mirror. 'Who is that? I don't recognise myself.'

'Well, I must say that I hardly recognise you either. But do you like it?'

'I'm not sure. I don't wear a lot of make-up. It takes a bit of getting used to.'

'The main thing is that the customers should like it. They expect us to look dramatic and beautiful. It would look strange to wear no make-up with our belly dance outfits.'

'I suppose you're right,' Gemma responded, still examining her face in the glass. She suddenly felt astounded and enthralled by her appearance: prettier, sexier, like a totally different person.

'OK, enough of your doubts. It's time to get dressed,' Fatima ordered, handing her the scarlet outfit.

'Aren't you going to dance?' Gemma asked, suddenly scared that she'd be the sole dancer.

'Don't worry. I'm going to prepare myself now. I wouldn't do that to you on your first night. Anyway, Mehmet Bey wants us both on the floor, mostly together but sometimes just one of us, while the other one stands by clapping.'

'Oh, right. That sounds OK.' Gemma watched as her friend expertly made up her face.

Fatima flicked through her outfits hanging on a rail. 'Hmm, I think I'll wear these orange pantaloons with matching sequinned top – they'll contrast well with your scarlet clothes.'

There was a knock on the door, then Mehmet Bey's voice. 'Are you ready, girls? May I come in?'

'Give us ten minutes,' Fatima said, quickly changing into her costume.

When she opened the door to her boss, he emitted a low whistle when he saw both her and Gemma. '*Çok, çok güzel,*' he breathed. 'You both look very beautiful.'

'*Teşekkür ederiz,*' Fatima responded, her eyes downcast, trying to suppress her giggles, while Gemma smiled, wondering if he actually meant it.

'The restaurant's filling up nicely so we'll begin the music soon. I think you, Fatima, should enter first, do a few rounds of the floor and then I'll knock on the door for you, Gemma. OK?'

Gemma nodded. There was no way that she was going to argue with her boss.

After Mehmet Bey had left, Fatima looked at Gemma and asked, 'Are you wearing contact lenses?'

'No. I had my glasses on when I came, remember? I've not had time to buy lenses,' she admitted. This was not strictly true. She had bad memories of trying out lenses a few years before. They had hurt her eyes and she wasn't keen to try again, especially in a foreign country.

'Oh dear! Well, you can't wear your glasses.'

'I suppose not. I'll just have to do a bit of peering,' Gemma joked.

'Please try not to,' Fatima said, frowning.

'Don't worry, Fatima. I'm not completely blind, you know,' said Gemma, trying to reassure her.

There was a sharp knock on the door. The girls looked at each other. 'Well, this is it,' said Fatima. 'Good luck, Gemma. I know you'll be fantastic.' And with that, she was out of the door.

Gemma perched on the make-up stool, listening to the music, imagining the customers stuffing notes into her friend's outfit. How would she feel? She didn't know and didn't care. She just wanted to dance and began to sway to the rhythm, moving her arms, trying out some of the hand movements Fatima had taught her.

There was a tap on the door – *her signal!* She felt a thrill pass through her and walked out onto the dance floor, smiling at the hazy blur in front of her. Fatima came close and whispered, 'Copy me.' Gemma closely followed her friend's twists and turns, her belly's undulations, her arm and hand movements as best she could. They were not close enough to the diners to receive tips, but then Fatima moved away, circulating the tables, allowing men – there were few women, to thrust notes into her costume. Gemma stood still, clapping her hands to the music's rhythm, trying to see how Fatima was doing. She noticed her stop at a far corner table for longer than usual, but could not make out who was sitting there.

Soon Fatima was dancing back to her. 'Your turn now,' she said, standing by her side. Then she swivelled towards the audience, raised her arms in the air and clapped her hands together. Gemma began to move slowly towards the tables, the blurred faces becoming clearer. She realised that she was getting a lot of attention and encouragement, presumably because she was a foreigner.

'*Gel, gel buraya, güzel kadın,*' one portly gentleman with a black, bushy moustache commanded, beckoning to her provocatively. His fat wife looked on approvingly as he fumbled in Gemma's bodice with his pudgy fingers, exhaling garlic-laden breath. Gemma smiled sweetly at him and then his partner, softly saying, '*Teşekkür ederim,*' much to their astonishment. She continued to play the tables, discovering that she was enjoying herself and not really minding the feeling of the notes being stuffed into her top and waistband. It helped that she could only clearly see the table she was performing at, the rest of the restaurant being a pleasant haze.

Eventually she found herself at the table in the far corner where Fatima had paused. A young man was sitting with a middle-aged couple. *Maybe his parents?* she wondered. There was a distinct resemblance between the younger and older man: they both had high foreheads, their glossy, black hair combed back, their large, dark eyes seeming to look deep down inside of her; their noses were large, but shapely, their chins square, their lips firm and pink. They were both handsome, the younger one moustache-less while the older man had a thin, black one. They seemed content to simply watch her dance, but then the woman, a fair-haired beauty with perfect features, pressed a large note into Gemma's palm, with a subtle blink of her right eye.

'Thank you,' Gemma said, switching to English, wondering what nationality the lady was.

'Thanks for your lovely dancing,' she replied in English with a Russian accent.

'You're very kind,' Gemma said politely, intrigued about the group's relationship.

The woman seemed to be equally interested in her. 'You're English, aren't you? Where did you learn to belly dance?'

'Fatima taught me, the other dancer over there.' Gemma turned to see her friend who was now playing the tables again.

The man looked appreciatively at Fatima. 'She's a remarkably good dancer, isn't she Can?'

The younger male nodded. 'We've been here before, haven't we father? We saw her dancing then.' Both the father and son spoke good English with Turkish accents, Gemma noticed.

At that moment Fatima danced nearer to Gemma and jerked her head. 'I'd better go,' said Gemma and followed her friend, who was heading towards her dressing room while the crowd applauded loudly, with shouts of, 'Bravo, bravo!'

*

Once inside the room Fatima said, 'I feel that's enough for this evening. They've had a double dose of dancing, after all.'

'Well, if you think that's OK,' Gemma said, wondering if Mehmet Bey would agree.

Fatima sensed her unspoken thought. 'Mehmet Bey won't mind, especially when I tell him who was here.'

Gemma noticed Fatima's nervous twisting of a piece of her long hair. 'What's wrong, Fatima? Is this something to do with the family at the corner table who you spoke to?'

Fatima sat down and shrugged, her mouth drooping disconsolately. Gemma sat next to her and took her hand. 'Please tell me,' she urged.

After a few minutes Fatima said, 'The man and boy came here a couple of months ago. They were with three other men, all wearing black suits, grey shirts and ties. They were sitting right at the front and made me nervous.'

'Why was that?' Gemma asked.

'It was partly the way they looked and behaved, but also because the boss had ordered me to wear my best costume and do my best dance moves beforehand.'

'Oh, I see. But why would he do that? I wonder who they were?'

'I don't know but afterwards they stayed chatting with Mehmet until late. Then, when they'd gone, he told me that they wanted me to give them a private show when they were next in town.'

'Well, that's not so bad, is it?'

'Not so bad! Maybe they want me to do more than just dance.'

'Oh, right.' Gemma felt stupid – how could she be so naïve?

'The worst thing was that Mehmet Bey said there would be repercussions if I refused.' Fatima's hair twisting increased. 'Then he said that they were extremely powerful people, so what can I do?'

'But you've not seen them again? Well, not until tonight, and it's different because it's only two of them, father and son, and the woman's probably the mother.'

'How do you know that?'

'Well, I know that they're father and son because they told me, but I'm guessing about the mother.'

'The boy doesn't look anything like her. She could be a Russian whore.'

'That's a horrible thing to say,' cried Gemma, then mused, 'she did have a Russian accent, though.'

'So, what did I say? Our country is overrun with Russian prostitutes. They come here and take our men – they love their fair skin and blonde hair. It's disgusting!'

There was a knock at the door. 'Come in,' shouted Fatima.

Mehmet Bey stood in the doorway, his mouth set in a stern line, a frown creasing his forehead. 'What's this? I've been out on business and when I come back I find the two of you in here chatting. You're supposed to be dancing, damn you!'

Fatima stood up and crossed her arms defiantly. 'We have been dancing. Both of us. Aren't we entitled to a break?'

Her boss's eyes flickered dangerously. 'If this is how you're going to behave when Gemma dances with you, I'll have to think again. Don't forget who pays your wages, young lady.'

'If it's money you want to talk about maybe you should join your friends in the corner,' Fatima said, her voice icy.

'What friends in the corner? I've just come in, I told you.'

'Go and see. There are two men with a blonde lady. The men were here before with three other men, remember?'

Mehmet stared at her. He did remember, but he wanted to forget. He had hoped they would never return. But maybe this was only a family outing. He would have to go and find out. He looked at his watch. 'OK, it's almost midnight. You girls can go home. How will you go, Gemma?'

Gemma had been watching him closely, aware of the change in his manner when Fatima had mentioned the people in the corner. His voice had softened and he tried to smile at her. 'I'll get a ferry across to Kadıköy.'

'No, no. You can't do that this late at night. You've probably missed the last one anyway.'

'She can come back with me,' said Fatima.

'OK. I'll order a taxi for you both.'

Gemma did not want to go with Fatima; she wanted to go home to her bed but she realised that it would be unsafe to attempt to go across the water and through the quiet streets alone.

'OK. If you're sure that's all right, Fatima?'

'Yes, I'm sure,' she replied, her dark eyes looking deep into Gemma's, making her feel uneasy.

SEVEN

Gemma sat on the Kadıköy ferry enjoying the fresh sea breeze. Yesterday evening's excitement, followed by a restless night on Fatima's lumpy sofa had left her feeling drained. Her friend had been sleeping when she left so she had scribbled a note to say that she would be in touch after Christmas.

It felt good to be back on the Asian side of the Bosphorus, *my home*, she thought, as she strode through the busy, narrow streets of the market towards her flat. On her arrival home Tina let out a relieved sigh. 'Where on earth have you been all night? I've been crazy with worry about you.'

'Oh, Tina. I'm really sorry but our dancing finished too late to catch the last ferry so I stayed at Fatima's.'

'Hmm. Well, you could have phoned.'

'I didn't want to disturb you. It was way after midnight by the time we got to Fatima's place.'

'OK. Well, I guess you're forgiven. How did it go anyway?'

'It was great! I loved every minute of it, except at the end when Fatima told me about a couple of guys who were there.' Gemma's radiant smile disappeared as she recalled her friend's nervousness.

'Hey! So spill the beans about the guys.' Tina plonked herself onto a kitchen chair and leant forward, all ears.

Gemma wished she hadn't mentioned the men – she didn't want to dwell on anything negative about her first wonderful public performance. 'Let's leave it, Tina. It was just something Fatima said. It's not important.'

'OK, if you say so, but I'll wheedle it out of you some time,' Tina said with a mischievous grin.

Gemma gave her a faint smile and changed the subject. 'So, are we definitely going to this *Termal* place for Christmas?' She had been dreaming about the hot springs, green forests and fresh air ever since she had heard about them.

'Sure, I'd love to go.'

'Let's go on Wednesday. Straight after breakfast,' said Gemma, 'then we'll get there at lunchtime.'

'Trust you, always thinking about your stomach.'

Gemma laughed, her spirits lifting at the thought of escaping the city. They didn't even need to book because it wasn't a Turkish holiday. Hasan had said there would be loads of places in the village of Gökçedere.

'Good, that's settled then.' Gemma gave a satisfied smile.

*

A murky mist hung over the sea as Gemma and Tina hurried towards Haydarpaşa train terminal. Its imposing, turreted façade dwarfed even the massive cranes and tankers in the nearby docks and when they entered they both gazed in awe at the high, patterned domed ceilings. The rush to work had passed and they easily found seats on the commuter train, although the floor was still littered and dirty from the morning's commute. They sat in silence, watching Istanbul's endless suburbs slowly slide past, block upon block of modern apartments, with only an occasional wooden mansion, surrounded by overgrown gardens, still standing in solitary splendour. The train stopped at every tiny station, allowing a few passengers to get on or off. They were accompanied by small boys, elderly men and women, selling things from the inevitable packets of tissues to complex kitchen gadgets which they skillfully demonstrated, keeping the occupants amused.

Finally, they reached Kartal station and shouldered their packs. Gemma was aware of the curious glances from alighting passengers and felt self-conscious, noticing that the obviously poor Turks surrounding them carried their possessions in former sugar sacks and battered plastic carrier bags. They passed a few old men sitting on stools outside the station. Some were busily typing out documents on manual typewriters for passers-by, while others sat patiently waiting for business. Gemma had been studying the sea bus timetable and they hoped to catch the next one, but as they sighted the sea they saw it speeding away. 'Damn! We'll have to get the ferry. The next sea bus is ages,' she moaned.

'Never mind. I like the ferries. We can walk around and look at the views.'

Gemma looked at the sea and then the sky. 'Hmm, well, the mist is lifting and it looks like the sun is trying to come out.'

'Great! I prayed for brilliant weather so I guess we're gonna get it.' Tina's positivity was infectious and soon Gemma was also looking forward to the boat trip.

When they reached the ferry terminal they saw from the timetable pasted on the wall that one was due in half-an-hour. They joined other passengers who were sitting on wooden benches lining the walls of the building. A *simit* seller stood outside the open door shouting, '*Buyuruz. Taze simit, taze, taze.*'

'Those sesame breads are making me hungry,' Tina said and went to buy one. She took a bite. 'Yuk! This tastes like sawdust. *Taze* my foot.'

Gemma chuckled. 'He'll have been here all morning shouting "fresh *simit*, fresh, fresh." We can get something on the boat – look! Here it comes.' Gemma peered through the spray splattered window.

'Let's go outside and wait. The sun's shining now,' Tina said.

They found an empty bench and watched as the tiny speck of the ship grew larger and larger. Soon it docked; hordes of passengers got off, stumbling across the rickety gangplanks laden with luggage. Once the ferrymen were certain that everyone had disembarked, the gates were opened and the Yalova-bound travellers streamed on. Gemma and Tina headed upstairs to the bufé and found a seat nearby. Tina bought them both a cheese toast and a glass of *Sahlep*.

'I love *Sahlep*,' said Gemma, sipping the thick and creamy drink. She tasted the cinnamon and felt the warmth slipping down her throat.

'We shouldn't really drink it, though. It's made from a rare orchid's root.'

'Oh, is that right?' Gemma said unhappily.

Once finished they went outside and walked around the deck, wrapping woollen scarves about their necks against the chilly breeze. From the rear of the ship Kartal and its environs were already fading into the distance. 'You can see from here how built-up Istanbul is,' said Gemma.

'It's horrible! Just a sprawling ugliness spreading up the hillsides. My students told me that the authorities can't control house building. Peasants arrive from the countryside and put up a makeshift home overnight. They call them *gecekondu*, which means "a house built in one night without permission",' Tina said.

The girls settled on a wooden bench which ran along the front deck against the windows. Turks sat silently smoking, brooding on serious matters, or at least this was how it seemed to Gemma, who observed that Turkish people when travelling were generally subdued. She tried not to encourage Tina to speak, because she was a typical American – chatty and loud. Any signs of hilarity could result in disapproving stares, or in unwelcome attention from unsavoury men, especially with her fair-skinned, blonde-haired prettiness. The distant purplish-grey mountains on the far side of the Sea of Marmara became closer and clearer. Soon green fields and forests could be seen, with a pleasing lack of buildings, except for the town of Yalova, which spread along the shoreline. The ferry's port was conveniently right in the centre and Tina and Gemma joined the bustling crowds heading for the town. Gemma looked around for a statue of Mustafa Kemal Atatürk, the first President and founder of the Turkish Republic. There was always one and sure enough there it was in the town square's centre, his hand raised in greeting.

Gemma paused and looked around. She spotted a large *lokanta* on the edge of the square. Her stomach rumbled. 'Let's go and grab a late lunch,' she suggested.

'So, you're not full of cheese toast?'

Gemma scowled. 'That was ages ago! We should eat here in case there isn't anywhere in the village.'

'OK. Let's do it. I'm starving.'

The restaurant was quiet as it was mid-afternoon. They put their packs down at a window table and went to look at the hot meals on display in large metal containers. They ordered portions of rice, green beans with tomatoes, aubergine stew, stuffed courgettes and yoghurt. The usual plate of crusty bread and bottles of water accompanied the food and soon they were tucking in, as if it were to be their last meal on earth. Once they'd finished they ordered *çay* and chatted to the manager who'd approached and asked all the usual questions, which they answered politely, being full of food and in good spirits. He told them where to get the minibus to the *Termal* and, promising to return on their way back, they found one which was waiting to fill up with passengers. Eventually the driver was satisfied that it was full and he drove around the centre, picking up a few more people, before heading out of town through orchards and hamlets. As usual fares were passed to the driver and Gemma clung to the seat, hardly daring to watch as he deftly steered with one hand while sorting fares and change with the other.

The road began to ascend into the hills. A reservoir lay spread out on the left hand side of the bus, another hamlet perched high on a ridge above it. After about twenty minutes a few houses appeared plus a couple of modern hotels and the driver shouted, 'Gökçedere.' Gemma and Tina got off then reached inside for their packs which had been squashed into a space near the door. They had expected there to be a few touts looking for business for their *pansiyonlar*, but there were none.

'So, what do we do now?' Tina asked.

The bus had stopped at the bottom of a hill. Gemma looked up the street which was lined with low rise buildings and said, 'I guess we go that way.'

'Yep – it looks like the only way to go,' agreed Tina. They began to trudge up the road, past a fruit and vegetable stall on one side, a *bufé* selling *pide* and *lahmacun*, the Turkish equivalent to pizza, on the other. A mini-market was further up and opposite was a two-storey building, a board outside proclaiming it to be the *Umut Pansiyon*. The girls stood surveying it.

'Shall we check it out?' Tina queried.

'Well, it looks OK and I like the name: *Hope Pansiyon* – I could do with some of that.'

While they'd been speaking a middle-aged man had come to the *pansiyon's* doorway. 'Are you looking for a room?' he asked.

'Yes, we are,' they both nodded and followed him inside to the reception desk, the usual framed photograph of Atatürk prominently displayed on the wall behind it. The price was ridiculously cheap compared with Istanbul's accommodation. The room itself was large, clean and basic, with two single beds, two wooden chairs, a table, a wardrobe with a few bent wire hangers and two bedside tables. The floor was stone and rug-less. There was a small toilet and shower cubicle. Tina felt the radiator: it was cold.

'Does your *kalorifer* work?' she asked the owner.

'Certainly, madam,' he assured her and bent to twist the control.

Tina was also obsessed with the lack of toilet rolls in most Turkish toilets, with the exception of upmarket hotels and restaurants.

Turkish loos were equipped with a tube which stuck out of the back, positioned at the anus, from which cold water would shoot out after turning a knob at the side. The only trouble was that the tube was often bent in the wrong position, the water too cold and the flow erratic. There was nothing to dry oneself with, hence the constant requirement for packets of tissues.

'May we have a toilet roll?' she enquired and the owner reluctantly agreed to supply one.

The formalities settled and their passports taken, they heaved their packs up the stairs. There was a spacious *balkon,* with a white plastic table and two chairs, and they sat watching as the village houses' lights came on, dusk falling fast. 'What do you fancy doing now?' Gemma asked.

'I'm not really hungry after our late lunch, so we could go for a wander.' Tina rubbed her legs which were feeling cold with the disappearance of the sun.

'Right. I'm not hungry either. Let's go and try to find the *Termal.*'

'Hmm. I could do with soaking in that hot water right now, but I guess it'll close soon.'

The owner told them that the baths were further up the road and then down a hill on the right at the top. It wasn't far, past another modern hotel, a few shops selling items for the baths: towels, swim wear, massage mitts, soaps and so on and a few small restaurants, which were almost empty. A wide path headed downhill, a wisteria-covered walkway with benches on one side, through the leafless branches of which they caught glimpses of steaming water, the sound of splashes and chatter wafting up, a faint sulphurous smell filling the air, mixed with a pungent, earthy aroma from the surrounding forest. They descended one of a pair of flights of steep, curving steps, with wide rails on either side supported by white pillars.

'Oh! Just look at that water,' Gemma breathed as the rectangular pool came into view. A few people were still sprawled on loungers, a line of changing cubicles on each side of the water. A large white dome with three windows overlooked the pool, a series of grey metal domes of different sizes rising up behind it.

'I guess you can go inside to the Turkish bath after your swim,' said Tina.

'Yes, I can't wait to get in that water. I wish we'd brought our swim gear.'

'Yeah, I didn't think it would be open so late,' Tina agreed. They walked across a bridge over a steaming stream which fed the baths. The five-star Termal Hotel, its large courtyard dotted with tables and chairs underneath the spreading branches of a huge tree came into view. 'Wow, this looks super lux,' Tina enthused.

'And super pricey,' Gemma added. They walked round the baths' domes to the pool's entrance. A noticeboard gave the times and prices.

'It's open until ten in the evening,' Tina gasped.

'So, we can wallow all day and night tomorrow,' Gemma laughed.

'Hmm. I'm not sure about that. We might dissolve.'

'Actually, you're not supposed to stay in the hot water too long.'

'Unfortunately, I think you're right,' said Tina, adding, 'I feel it's bedtime. How about you?'

Gemma agreed and they returned to their room, made cosy with the heating, and were soon sleeping, dreaming of sulphurously steaming pools.

EIGHT

The girls woke up slowly the next morning, aware of the sun's rays shining through a gap in the curtains. They skipped showering as they planned to have a thorough wash in the Turkish bath. The owner, who had told them his name was Murat, ushered them to a table by the window in his small restaurant. The breakfast was on the meagre side with no boiled eggs, only a few black olives, slices of cucumber and tomato and a piece of white cheese, to accompany the plentiful supply of white bread. They drank glasses of *çay* and watched the few passers-by, who appeared to be mostly locals.

'It's not much like Christmas Eve, is it?' Tina remarked.

'No, it isn't. No sign of last minute frantic shopping, Christmas decorations or trees.'

'Actually, I think I like it. Christmas has become so commercialised in the States, all folk think about is buying stuff that they don't need and eating and drinking to excess.'

'You're right. It's the same in the UK. This feels really refreshing. I'm so glad that we decided to come here.'

Soon they were walking back up the street but stopped when they smelt the delicious smell of baking. 'Let's go in here and get snacks for the pool,' Tina said. The rotund, cheerful baker and his equally fat wife greeted them warmly, keen to chat. They answered their questions expertly, their Turkish for giving basic information about themselves well practised. As they left, clutching bags of savoury pastries and floury shortbread, the baker and his wife cried, '*güle, güle,*' to their farewell of '*iyi günler.*'

There was a small queue at the pool's entrance and the girls waited their turn expectantly, already feeling invigorated by the fresh, clean air and verdant surroundings. They received large, white towels in return for their money and descended steps down to the poolside. '*Hoş geldiniz,*' a stockily-built attendant with brown hair, a thin moustache and hazel eyes, greeted them warmly, locked away their valuables and showed them to two adjacent cubicles. They quickly changed into their swimsuits and grabbed two loungers, on which they draped their towels.

'Now for the pool,' Gemma said, carefully climbing down the steep ladder. 'Oh! It's so hot!' she squealed as her feet touched the water. She slowly submerged herself in the water's warmth, feeling it penetrating her whole body, her muscles relaxing, her tensions forgotten. Tina quickly followed and they both floated, suspended timelessly, gazing up at the blue sky, across which a few puffy white clouds were passing. Palms bordered one side of the pool with deciduous trees rising behind the private baths building on the other, while coniferous and broad-leaved forests covered distant hills. Gemma swam a couple of lengths, then paused for breath. Tina bobbed up beside her.

'It's too hot for swimming,' Gemma said.

'Too right! I'm going out to cool down,' Tina replied, climbing up the ladder. They both lay on their loungers in the cool air, feeling too hot to wrap themselves in their towels. Gemma sat up and put on her glasses to see some new people arriving. Something about them caught her attention: a middle-aged man with dark hair, a blonde woman and a younger man, who bore a resemblance to the older male. *Where had she seen them before?* Suddenly she remembered: the corner table in the restaurant as she danced towards them. *What a strange coincidence.*

Tina sat up, wrapping her towel around her, beginning to feel cold. 'Who are you staring at?' she asked Gemma.

Gemma turned to look at her, a mixture of excitement and anxiety on her face. 'It's those people from the restaurant – the ones I told you about, remember?'

'Oh, the father and son and the Russian whore?'

'Yes, but don't say that. She's probably totally respectable. It was Fatima who called her a whore.' Gemma watched as the attendant showed them to some cubicles, seeing the older man press something into his hand. *A tip?* She supposed. Tina reached for her book but Gemma continued to stare at their cubicle doors, her heart pounding expectantly. She was rewarded by the sight of the father first, his bulk surprisingly muscular, his chest covered in a thick mass of straight, black hair, a gold medallion round his neck. He was wearing dark blue boxer shorts and immediately entered the pool which he swam across slowly. The son emerged next, clad in close-fitting black trunks, his buttocks perfectly moulded, as was the rest of his slim, broad-shouldered body. Gemma felt a thrill pass through her, something she had not felt for some time. The lady pushed open her door last. She was wearing a low cut white bikini, which showed off her perfect curves, her smooth, honey-coloured skin shining in the sunlight. She had tied up her long, blonde hair with a turquoise chiffon scarf. She lay down on her lounger and closed her eyes.

Soon the son joined his father in the pool. Gemma stood up, propelled by something uncontrollable. 'Are you going in again already?' Tina asked.

'Yes.' Gemma could only manage a monosyllabic reply.

'Oh, right. I get it. Be careful,' Tina said. *Be careful of what?* Gemma thought as she climbed down the steps into the water. Her heart was hammering as she edged her way around the pool to where the father and son were standing, deep in conversation. When she was a short distance away from them she floated around for a while, hoping to attract their attention. She righted herself and almost brushed against the father.

'Pardon,' she said, embarrassed at their closeness, noticing a jagged white scar running down his neck.

'*Problem yok*,' said the father with a wide grin, exposing his bright white glinting teeth, while his son stared hard at Gemma, whose face, already red from the heat, grew even redder.

'Don't I know you?' he asked her in English.

Gemma fixed a surprised look onto her face and looked at him closely. 'I'm not sure but you do look familiar,' she said, keen to prolong their encounter.

'I know what it is! You were belly dancing in that restaurant off İstiklal Caddesi.'

Gemma appeared suitably astonished. 'Oh, yes, I remember now. Your name's Can, isn't it?'

'Yes, and this is my father, Serkan.'

Serkan Bey politely said, 'I'm pleased to meet you again. What is your name?'

'Gemma.' Gemma smiled at them both, pleased with how the situation was going.

'Gemma. That's a pretty name. Do you know what it means?' asked Can.

'I'm sorry, I don't.'

'I'm sure it has a beautiful meaning,' said Can. 'Mine means "soul or life" and Serkan means "chief or leader."'

'They're great names and now I've learnt two more Turkish words. I ask my students what their names mean – it's a good way to increase my vocabulary.'

'So, you are not really a belly dancer but a teacher?' said Can, raising his eyebrows, a wry smile on his lips.

'Of course, I am an English teacher. I'm here with my flatmate, Tina. We both work in a language school in Kadıköy.'

'Oh, I see, so you can teach me some English for exchange of my Turkish,' Can suggested.

Gemma had heard this many times before: it was employed by Turkish men as a possible way into a relationship. She generally ignored it, or laughed it off but this time she heard herself saying, 'That's a good idea. Where do you live?'

Can immediately became distant, upsetting Gemma with his vague reply of, 'I'm between addresses at the moment,' which accompanied a strange look that passed between him and his father. Then, as if to make amends, he issued an invitation, 'Would you and your friend like to join me for a drink tonight? We're staying at the Termal Hotel.'

Gemma needed no time to think about this. 'I'd love to but I'll need to ask Tina.' She looked over to Tina's lounger. She was sitting watching so Gemma swam across to ask her.

When she heard the invitation she asked, 'Are you sure you want me to be there?'

'Yes, absolutely! I don't entirely trust these people,' Gemma whispered.

'It all sounds most mysterious so count me in; I love mysteries,' Tina said, her voice hardly audible above the poolside babble.

Gemma returned to Can and Serkan with the news. 'That's great! Let's say eight o'clock in the bar,' Can said. 'We're going inside now for a scrub and massage, so we'll see you this evening.'

*

Gemma got out of the water and went to sit beside Tina. 'So, that's settled. We're meeting them at eight.'

'What do you mean by "them"?'

'Well, I guess it means all three of them, but I'm not sure.' Gemma looked across to where the lady was still reclining on her lounger, unaware of all their activity.

'Oh well, it'll all become clear tonight.'

They spent another couple of hours lounging, reading and swimming, nibbling at their snacks and drinking lots of water. The lady had got up and gone into the bath, emerging with the men just as Gemma and Tina were thinking of going inside. All three were pink and glowing as they entered their cubicles and gave the girls a wave as they left. 'Do you fancy going inside?' Gemma asked.

'Yeah, sure. We've still got plenty of time.' They put their things in their cubicles and went up the steps, past the entrance and then down another flight of steps to the heavy wooden door of the Turkish bath. They pushed it open and were greeted by the same smiling attendant who gave them more towels and a pair of wooden flip-flops with canvas straps, which they found most awkward to wear. The man warned that the marble floor inside was 'çok sıcak' – very hot, and they nodded at him, passing the squat-style toilets, from which there was a strong stink of urine and then through another wooden door into the bath. The heat was intense, the air steamy, with a strong sulphurous smell mixed with sweat. As their eyes became accustomed to the atmosphere, they saw a shaft of light shining down from the high dome. There was a large pool, where several people, mostly male, were sitting clad in baggy swimming trunks. It was, unusually for Turkey, a mixed sex Turkish bath, so bathers had to be clothed, unlike the segregated ones where nudity was the norm. A cloth was wrapped around the body after washing in these establishments. On each side of the water were alcoves with steep marble steps down, on which one person sat, pouring water over themselves from a metal bowl which was filled from a gushing tap. After wetting themselves they rubbed their skin hard with a rough cloth, finishing with a soapy wash and ending with another rinse. Couples rubbed each other's backs and possibly other bodily parts – the alcoves were partly obscured by steam, making it difficult to see. At the far end was another heavy wooden door. This led into the sauna. The girls managed to go in but quickly came out, feeling as if they had been fried. 'How can anyone stand that heat?' Gemma wanted to know, swigging water from her bottle.

In the centre, on the floor, was a scalding hot, small round pool.

A man lay spread-eagled at its edge being massaged by a big, burly man. His limbs were pulled in all directions as he groaned loudly and the masseur uttered guttural cries. 'If that's massage there's no way I'm having it! It looks more like torture,' Tina cried.

Gemma and then Tina carefully entered the big pool, making sure to keep their distance from the wallowing males. 'This is too hot! I don't think I can stand it for very long,' Tina said.

'It is a bit overwhelming,' Gemma agreed and then said wistfully, 'I'd love to get a relaxing massage though.'

'I'm not sure if they do that,' Tina said. 'You'd want to make sure that it wasn't that masseur by the floor pool – he'd pull you apart!'

Gemma decided to go out and ask the attendant. 'Watch yourself,' Tina warned. Wrapping herself in her towel Gemma stumbled along on the ridiculous shoes until she reached the bath's reception desk. The friendly attendant was there so she asked him if it were possible to have a massage.

'Of course. I can give you one now if you like,' he replied with a smile. Gemma was rather taken aback. She had thought there would be special people performing massage, with a female masseur for the ladies.

'How much is it?' she asked.

'*Para yok*,' was his reply, accompanied by the subtle teeth click, eyebrow and head raise, which meant absolutely that no money was involved.

This confused Gemma even more, but she felt at ease with this man, with his kind, hazel eyes and heard herself saying, 'OK.'

He instantly handed over the desk to another worker, produced a clean towel, rough mitten cloth and bar of soap and led Gemma back into the bath, then through into a large side area, which she hadn't previously noticed. There was a massage table in the centre of the floor and an alcove with steps at the far end. He motioned her towards the alcove and they descended the steps where they were partially hidden from view. He wanted her to stand, so she stood meekly, facing away from the room, while he turned on the ornate brass handle of the tap. Hot water gushed out. He wetted the cloth, then rubbed it with soap. He began to rub Gemma's shoulders hard, then her arms and hands. He began to move the straps of her swimsuit down and she remained motionless, allowing him to do it. He rubbed the upper half of her breasts, then lowered the swimsuit more so that he could do the lower half and then her belly. It was an exquisite sensation. She felt a strange mix of emotions: on one level she felt like a baby being lovingly washed by its mother, while on another she was extremely sexually aroused. Next he told her to sit on a step while he rubbed her back, and then her legs and feet. His breath was hot and laboured, with a faint whiff of garlic, his sweat almost sweet. She vaguely realised that he was aroused – maybe even more than her. The rubbing and scrubbing finished he ordered her to stand while he poured dish after dish of hot water over her head and body. She noticed layers of dirty skin sloughing off of her and he commented that she'd been, '*cok kirli*,' very dirty, which made her feel slightly ashamed.

The next stage of the procedure involved an actual massage. She sat on the table where he told her to lie down on her front. She had pulled the top of her swimsuit back up but once again he began to pull it down to access her back and then her buttocks. She wriggled warningly, looking over her shoulder at the entrance but was calmed by his wonderfully expressive, '*Yok*.' This one utterance could convey such a wealth of meaning and was her favourite Turkish word. His broad hands glided over her oiled body, relaxing her muscles and making her feel even more aroused. His hands never ventured near her private parts – they didn't need to. She rolled onto her back, his hands once more gliding and kneading as if she was a lump of dough. He stretched out each of her hands in his and tugged, causing her to cry out. Finally, he lightly pummelled her with the edges of his hands, up and down her back and the backs of her legs. He stood upright. '*Bitti*,' he announced. It's finished. Gemma hoisted herself off of the table, her whole body aglow, her legs feeling like rubber. He wrapped the clean, fluffy white towel around her and led her out into the foyer, where he gave her a towelling robe. She learnt that Tina was sitting waiting in the small café, further down the corridor. She was reclining on a lounger, also wrapped in a robe and drinking *çay*.

'There you are at last,' she smirked giving her flatmate a knowing look.

'I'm sorry, Tina. I've no idea what time it is.'

'Look, there's a clock there on the wall.'

'Five o'clock! I can't believe it – I must have been in there about an hour.' Gemma sat ruminating on how time runs away when one is experiencing immense pleasure. She ordered some *çay* and a bottle of water and sat quietly thinking about her first Turkish massage, the memory of his touch still strong.

'Well, it sure looks as if you enjoyed your massage with that dreamy look on your face,' Tina chuckled.

Gemma went red and muttered, 'Yes, it was pretty good.'

'OK. I guess I'm not going to get the lurid details any time soon. We'd better get a move on. We don't want to be late for your date.'

'What do you mean, "date"? It's just a meeting, that's all.'

'Right, if you say so,' said Tina, getting up. 'Let's go and get changed.'

*

As Gemma sat waiting on a bench near the entrance for her friend her masseur appeared. 'Will you be coming here again?' he asked.

Gemma tried not to smile too widely. 'Maybe, I'm not sure,' she said, thinking, *for sure I will.*

At that moment Tina came up the steps and gave them both a quizzical look. 'Are you ready to go now, Gemma?'

'Yes, of course,' said Gemma, wishing the attendant, '*iyi geceler.*'

'Hmm, it looks like you've got yourself a hot date here,' Tina remarked as they walked along the path.

Gemma blushed. 'Don't be daft. It was only a massage,' she said defensively.

'If you say so. Anyway, I'm starving. Do you fancy getting a *lahmacun*?'

'That's a good idea. We don't really have time to go to a restaurant.'

'No, we don't. I wonder whose fault that is?'

'OK, enough!' laughed Gemma. They went to the *bufé* and ordered two *lahmacun*, the smell of the baking dough, topped with minced meat and vegetables, garlic, parsley and spices, increased their hunger, making their mouths water. Once baked in an open brick oven the Turkish style pizzas were covered with fresh, flat-leaved parsley and sprinkled with lemon juice, finally being wrapped in paper. The girls hurried to their *pansiyon*, keen to tuck in as soon as possible. Murat Bey was sitting outside and they exchanged greetings with him before going to their room. They put the food on the *balkon* table, along with glasses of water, and ate the tasty *lahmacun* with their hands, wrapping pieces around the parsley, before shoving them into their mouths. Silence reigned until they were finished.

'Hmm, that was delicious,' sighed Gemma.

'It sure was. I feel more like sleeping now than going to the bar.'

'I know what you mean. I feel the same, it's all that soaking in hot water, it makes you tired, but we'd better go.'

'OK. I'm dying to find out more about these mysterious people anyway. I guess we'd better freshen up first,' Tina said reluctantly.

Both girls quickly got ready and changed into clean tops to go with their jeans. Gemma looked at her watch. 'Time to go,' she said with a twinge of nervous excitement. Murat Bey was still sitting outside and observed them closely as they left.

'Do you ever get the feeling that you're being watched?' Tina said.

'All the time. They're so damn inquisitive'. She liked Turkish people a lot, but not their nosiness, although coming from a small English village she had experienced something similar.

They soon reached the *Termal* Hotel and found the bar where Can was sitting on a stool chatting to the bar man. He stood up when he saw them and a strong smell of expensive after shave wafted over them, as they took in his attire. Gone was the black suit, tie and grey shirt. In their place he wore a neatly pressed pair of tightly-fitting denims and an open-necked navy-blue shirt. Gemma felt her heart lurch as her eyes met his and he extended his hand in greeting. She would have preferred the Turkish kisses on both cheeks but guessed it was too early in their acquaintance to do this. 'Thank you both for coming,' he said with a charming smile and ushered them to a corner table by the window, which had a view of the floodlit, empty courtyard. Their polite greetings over he asked, 'What would you girls like to drink?' They both requested Turkish gin and tonics, with lots of ice. 'Are you sure you wouldn't prefer imported gin?' he asked.

'We like the Turkish kind – it has a great taste,' Tina said. Can raised his eyebrows, then summoned a waiter. He ordered imported whisky for himself, on the rocks.

Once their drinks arrived Gemma asked, 'Where are your

parents?'

'They're not my parents,' he admitted.

'Oh, I thought Serkan Bey was your father?' Gemma said, feeling embarrassed.

'Well, Serkan is my dad but Natalia is a colleague. They're in a meeting right now.'

Tina butted in, 'On Christmas Eve?'

Can shrugged. 'Christmas is not important in Turkey.'

'Yes, but Natalia's Russian isn't she?' Tina said.

Can began to look annoyed and Gemma frowned at Tina. *This was not going well,* she thought.

'She is Russian but she's in Turkey,' Can said patiently to Tina, a look of dislike on his face.

'We understand that, don't we Tina?' Gemma said, then tried to change the subject. 'What do you do, Can?'

Can took a swig of whisky, the appearance of his dark eyes turning from annoyed to shifty. 'I'm in finance,' he said sternly, then caught a waiter's attention and ordered another drink.

Gemma decided to drop the subject and kept quiet, stirring and sipping her gin, hoping that Tina would have the sense not to ask him any more irritating questions. Her flatmate attempted another, hopefully safer, change of subject. 'So, you met Gemma when she was belly dancing?' she asked and Can's expression relaxed.

'Yes, I did. She dances very well and so does Fatima, the other dancer,' he said, draining his glass. 'Would you like another drink?' he asked, then ordered two more gins and a whisky, along with a bowl of assorted nuts. Gemma was glad to have something to nibble, but the nuts' saltiness made her thirsty, so she asked for a glass of water and decided to stick with it, observing that Can was looking rather drunk. She wondered about his secretiveness, his inability to answer simple questions, like where he lived and what his job was. Tina was right, there was a mystery.

Tina excused herself and went to the toilet. As soon as she'd gone Can leant close to Gemma and almost whispered, 'Gemma, I'm worried about Fatima, she's your friend, isn't she?'

'Yes, she is,' Gemma said, suddenly alert.

Can's glance swept furtively around the bar. *What's he afraid of?* Gemma wondered.

He seemed to make a decision and leant even closer. 'There are some people, some men, who want to use your friend in, shall we say, illegal activity. When I saw Fatima I felt close to her – do you know what I mean?' Gemma reluctantly realised that she did know what he meant. Her fantasies about him suddenly collapsed. She nodded and Can continued, 'I want to protect her but I don't know how to. I'm too involved myself. Can you warn her that she's in danger?'

'I can do that but can't you tell me more?'

Can saw Tina approaching and hurriedly hissed, 'No, I can't.' He moved away from Gemma as Tina sat down, and then excused himself.

'My, you two were getting real close,' Tina observed with a chuckle.

'It's not what you think. I'll tell you later but I think we should go now.'

'OK, but shouldn't we wait for Can?'

'Here he is now,' Gemma said and turned to Can. 'We're really tired, Can, so we need to leave now. Thanks for the drinks.'

'Oh, right. Not at all, it was my pleasure,' Can said, switching into politeness. Tina put her jacket on and began heading for the door. 'Let me help you with your coat,' Can said to Gemma, muttering, 'please help her,' as he slipped his card into her pocket.

*

The frosty air revived the girls as they strolled back to their *pansiyon*. The sky was clear and full of stars. Tina gazed upwards. 'It makes me feel how insignificant I am,' she observed.

'Yes, we are insignificant but I can't help worrying about what Can said.'

'So, what did he say?'

Gemma looked around, suddenly scared. 'I'll tell you once we're safe in our room.'

'Wow! You've got me real curious now.'

Murat Bey was sitting smoking inside the *pansiyon* on their return. He greeted them politely, obviously making an effort not to ask them where they had been. They hurried to their room where Tina immediately began her own interrogation of Gemma. 'So, the gorgeous Can fancies Fatima – too bad for you,' she said.

'Is that all you can say?' Gemma said, her face creasing up with irritation.

'Whoa – what's riling you?'

'The fact that he fancies Fatima is irrelevant. She's my friend and she's in danger,' Gemma said in a hushed, but urgent voice.

Tina gave her flatmate a perplexed look. 'You're acting as if there's someone listening at the door. Get a grip, Gemma.'

'Listen, Tina. Those men are probably gangsters. Mehmet Bey told Fatima that they were powerful and there would be repercussions if she didn't perform for them – it's not funny.'

'OK, so they're the Turkish Mafia – what are you going to do about it?'

Gemma bit her lower lip nervously. 'I don't know, but I must tell Fatima.'

'OK, tell her, then stop seeing her and stop dancing at that restaurant.'

'I don't know if I can do that. I really like Fatima and I love to belly dance in front of an audience. It was incredible.'

'Well, it's up to you, but it might get just a bit too incredible.' Tina stood up and yawned. 'I'm real tired, let's go to bed. We can talk more about this tomorrow – it's Christmas Day, remember?'

'You're right. I'm tired too,' said Gemma with a sigh.

'Hey, cheer up! We'll have a lovely time tomorrow and forget about all this intrigue.'

'OK, it's a deal,' said Gemma, and in no time they were both asleep.

*

'Merry Christmas!' Gemma reluctantly opened her eyes to see Tina standing beside her bed holding out a present.

'Merry Christmas to you too,' Gemma said, yawning widely.

'Sorry to waken you, but I couldn't wait any longer. I'm always like this Christmas morning, and it's a white one, too!'

Gemma peered through the net curtains to see large snowflakes slowly falling. 'Oh, how wonderful!' she cried, pulling off her bed covers with a shiver. 'The heating's not on much, is it?' she moaned as she put on a jumper and headed for the bathroom. On emerging she handed Tina her present.

'Oh, thank you! Let's open them together,' Tina enthused.

They sat side by side on Gemma's bed, carefully undoing the wrapping paper. They looked at each other's gifts and burst out laughing. Each held a leather-bound Turkish diary for 1993. Both pleased with their presents they went down to breakfast, where Murat Bey surprised them with an '*Iyi Noeler.*' They returned his Christmas greeting and were treated to boiled eggs with their breakfast.

By the time they had finished eating it had stopped snowing. 'Shall we go back to the pool today?' Tina asked, aware that they would need to leave late afternoon to return to Istanbul on the sea bus.

'Yes, I'd like that but we could go for a walk first.'

'OK, let's do that,' Tina agreed. They were glad of their warm coats and boots when they ventured outside. The sky was leaden and they walked briskly towards the pool, which was completely hidden by steam. A light covering of wet snow covered the path which led into the forest, following the stream, which was hot in places with steamy clouds hovering over it. The trees were powdered with snow and a few birds called from their high branches, piercing the still air with their song. There was no sign of any people, no Christmas merriment, but the girls felt content just to be in that special place.

After a short time the path petered out, the forest-covered hills spreading into the distance. 'Let's go and warm up,' Gemma said.

'Sure. That hot water is definitely beckoning.'

There was a different attendant on the gate, Gemma noted with some disappointment as they received their towels and went to change. 'Oh, it's too cold for this,' Tina squealed as she undressed, then quickly entered the steaming water, along with Gemma, both of their bodies immediately becoming blissfully warm. They floated around, losing each other in the steam. They seemed to be the sole occupants of the pool and revelled in it. 'No sign of the lovely Can or his dodgy dad and mistress,' Tina commented as they stretched out together.

'No, and I'm quite relieved; in fact it's a huge relief to have the place to ourselves. Imagine if there were any sleazy Turkish men in here now, they'd use the steam as an excuse to bump into us.'

'Too right,' agreed Tina. They both wallowed for a little longer, then lay on their loungers to cool down, before immersing themselves yet again. The time slipped effortlessly by and soon they had to dress and reluctantly left, catching a minibus from the *Termal's* gate. The snow became less and less and by the time they reached sea level it was completely gone. Back in Yalova they ate in the same *lokanta*, then headed for the sea bus terminal where they managed to board the last one going to Kartal. It was an altogether modern and comfortable experience, compared with the ferry, the bus zooming over the water, and in no time they were disembarking in Kartal, the noise of the crowds and the air pollution hitting them both, the *Termal* seeming already like a far off dream.

NINE

Fatima awoke late to find that Gemma had gone. '*I'll be in touch after Christmas,*' she read and wondered how her dear friend was feeling. She had danced beautifully and had even seemed to enjoy receiving money from the customers. She had dutifully given it to Mehmet Bey, who had taken his cut, returning a small wad of notes to her, just as he did with Fatima. She made herself a cup of strong coffee and sat at her kitchen window, cradling it in her hands, watching a pack of stray, mangy dogs tearing at a rubbish bag in the narrow street below. She remembered her conversation with the young man, his father and the Russian woman. They had commented on her Kurdish accent and she had felt forced to admit that she was from the eastern border. It had made her feel even more vulnerable, especially as the younger man's eyes had searched her own so deeply she felt that he had touched her soul. The father had praised her dancing and had said, '*We look forward to your private performance soon, Fatima.*' Her stomach churned at the memory. *How soon was soon?* she wondered.

Fortunately, she had the day off and decided to relax, as far as it was possible. She began with a long soak, glad that the water supply was on that day. She hated the fact that Istanbul suffered from regular water cuts and she had to store bottles and tubs of it for the days when it was switched off. She lay submerged in bubbles, her eyes closed, willing her mind to empty. It was impossible. She really needed to visit Hudai's tomb, where she would be able to find peace, but she couldn't stand the stress of battling through the crowded streets and onto the ferries that day. The memory of the tissue seller's face, identical to her own, swam into her head. *Would she ever see her again*?

It was a fine, but chilly day and Fatima strolled through a small park near her tiny flat in Fatih, a poor neighbourhood on the other side of the Golden Horn from İstiklal Caddesi. Pre-school children slid down slides and swung high on swings, pushed by their mums.

Fatima felt a pang as she watched their play – *would she ever be a mother?* With her past, she doubted that this could ever happen. At the far end of the park was a *pastahane*, a little pastry shop and café, where she ordered a large slice of rich chocolate gateaux and a coffee. Normally she controlled her calorie intake, anxious to keep her figure, but on that day her need for comfort food was too great. If she hadn't given up smoking she would have had a cigarette instead. Next she wandered across the street and bought a woman's magazine, then sat on a park bench and thumbed through its pages of glamorous-looking women wearing too much make-up, complicated food recipes and, on the final page, the horoscope. She was an airy Aquarian and always avidly read her stars. The one for that day promised money and a new romance, but warned her to take care. She closed her eyes and tried to fantasise about the young man with deep, dark eyes in the restaurant, but Gemma's peering eyes, without her glasses, kept getting in the way. She needed to escape into another world and went to watch a romantic film at the cinema which had a predictable happy ending. That night her dreams were more like nightmares, intensely muddled, the threat of something intangible hovering over them.

*

The next night the restaurant was busy with professional types winding down after a hard week's work, plus a smattering of tourists. Fatima was kept busy working the tables, receiving a generous number of notes stuffed hotly into her waistband, bodice and even stuck on her forehead with a lick of saliva. At the end of the evening when she gave Mehmet Bey the money he said, 'Please can you stay for a few minutes? I have something important to tell you.'

Fatima looked at his worried face. 'Yes, of course,' she said, sitting down on her make-up stool. She watched him with concern: he was still standing, nervously picking the backs of his hands.

He fixed his anxious gaze on her and took a deep breath. 'You remember those five men who were here some time ago?'

'Yes,' replied Fatima, filled with foreboding.

'And then two of them returned with a Russian woman when Gemma was dancing?'

'Yes,' she said again. *How could she forget?*

'They had come to speak with me and stayed after I had shut the restaurant. The older man, Serkan Bey, seems to be the leader, the most powerful of all of them.'

'So, who are they and who is the Russian lady?' Fatima interrupted.

'Please don't interrupt. Let me explain, Fatima. As you are so interested in the woman, I can only say what I have surmised – that she is a link to a Russian network.'

Fatima again interjected, 'A network of what? And is she a whore?'

Mehmet sighed. 'She may well be a "whore" as you say, but I think that she's Serkan Bey's "property", so to speak, as well as being a useful business contact.'

He regarded Fatima, her unspoken question, *What business?* hanging in the air. 'This is hard for me to explain, Fatima. I hope you are able to have sympathy for me.'

'That depends,' Fatima said.

Mehmet lit a cigarette, his hands shaking slightly. He exhaled carefully, avoiding Fatima's gaze. 'The business is drug dealing and smuggling,' he said and waited for a reaction.

'What kind of drugs?' Fatima did not look at all surprised.

'Mostly heroin,' he admitted.

'So, the hard stuff – fantastic!'

'What do you mean, "fantastic?"'

'It's where the money is – you can become rich, Mehmet Bey!'

'Listen to me, Fatima. I do not want to do this; I do not want the money; I only want my life and my family's security. If I do not do what they want, I will not have these things.'

Fatima sat silently, letting the meaning of his words penetrate. She had been right to fear those men, but she was strong, stronger than them and she could get the better of them.

'What are you thinking about, Fatima?'

'I am thinking that I am stronger than these men, these criminals.'

Mehmet Bey gave a hollow laugh. 'Are you crazy? How can you be stronger than the Mafia?'

'Just wait and see, my dear boss. Just wait.'

'My dear, you are talking nonsense. I am only telling you this because Serkan Bey instructed me to. They want you to play a central role in the operation.'

'What on earth do you mean, a central role?'

'They love your belly dancing and they want to liven up their actual dealing by using your dancing.'

'How will that work? Will they stuff packets of heroin into my bodice?' Fatima laughed uproariously.

'Exactly so! How did you know this?'

'It was a joke! I was only joking.'

'Some joke. This is dangerous work, Fatima. I don't want your life to be in danger but they've got me in their grasp. If I refuse to participate they would wreck my business and possibly my life.'

'I see. Well, I do feel some sympathy for you, but I still believe that the righteous – that's us, are stronger and we can win.'

'I wish with all my heart that you are right, my dear, but how can this be achieved?'

'By prayer and trust in God.'

'You are a believer?' Mehmet Bey said incredulously.

'Indeed I am.'

*

A week passed by with no further developments. Fatima continued to belly dance as usual while her boss was distant towards her. On Christmas Day she visited Hudai's tomb and prayed hard for strength and help. She became calm and peaceful in his presence and left with a feeling that everything was perfectly in place.

Two days after Christmas Gemma phoned her. 'Oh, Gemma, I'm so pleased to hear your voice. How was your trip?'

'Wonderful! The *Termal* is such a beautiful place – we should go together some time.'

'Yes, I would like that.'

'What are you doing for New Year?'

'I shall be working New Year's Eve, unfortunately.'

'Oh, that's too bad. We're going to have a party in our flat with some friends and students.'

'I wish I could come but it's a big night at the restaurant. What about New Year's Day?' She was relieved when Gemma agreed to meet her in Kadıköy that evening. As she put the phone down she realised how much she had missed her friend, simultaneously grasping that she would have to stop her belly dancing in the restaurant: it was too dangerous.

*

Mehmet Bey was sitting chain smoking by the window when Fatima arrived at the restaurant New Year's Eve. He jumped up when she entered and followed her into her room. His face was ashen and he went straight to what was troubling him. 'Fatima, those people are coming tonight, so please take special care with your clothes and make-up and perform your best dance moves. They'll be sitting at the front again so give them lots of attention.'

'Of course I will do my best, Mehmet Bey. Do you think anything else will happen tonight?'

'Anything else? I doubt it, it's New Year and I assume that they are here simply to celebrate.'

'I hope you are right,' Fatima said, twisting a lock of her hair nervously.

'Please don't be anxious, and don't show them that you are. I'm sure everything will be all right.'

'Tonight maybe, but what about later?'

'I'm sorry, but I cannot tell. I just do what I'm told, and you must do the same,' her boss said sternly. With that he left, leaving her to get ready, which she did, trying hard to relax.

The signal for her to begin came and she entered the restaurant, wearing a stunning, emerald green sequinned bodice and long, split-sided skirt. Her bare feet had red-varnished toe nails and her glossy, black hair was coiled over her shoulder. The place was packed and decorated with glittery paper chains and multi-coloured balloons. Right in front of the dance floor was the group she had no desire to see. The same five men were there, attired in more festive clothes: smart trousers and open-necked expensive-looking shirts. Serkan Bey was accompanied by Natalia, whose blonde hair was loose around her shapely shoulders. She wore a tight-fitting, long black sleeveless satin dress, cut low to reveal her deep cleavage. Around her neck was a gold pendant, with golden bracelets on her slender wrists and a large diamond sparkled on the ring finger of her left hand. The other three older men all had beautiful women sitting next to them. Only Can was single, Fatima noticed as she danced for them, flashing him a sexy smile. He could not stop looking at her, while the others busily chatted as they nibbled their *meze* and sipped their drinks.

Midnight came and there was an orgy of kissing and hugging. Can reached Fatima before anyone else and slowly planted kisses, first on one cheek and then the other. He went to kiss her scarlet lips, but she quickly turned away her head. He hissed in her ear, 'I must talk to you,' but Fatima only smiled and walked away, heading towards the bathroom. After midnight customers began to leave, but a few, including the group, remained, drinking steadily. Fatima continued to dance until Mehmet Bey told her to stop. He ordered her a taxi and she hurried to her room, desperate to leave. She slipped her bracelets off and was in the middle of removing her costume when there was a knock on the door.

'Give me a minute,' she said, thinking it was her taxi, but instead, without waiting, Serkan Bey entered. She gasped, aware of his eyes travelling over her body as she flung on her coat, one shoe off, the other dangling.

Serkan's face was inscrutable as he spoke. 'Just a quick word, Fatima. We know about your background, your family. We know why you came alone to Istanbul, so please don't let us down.'

'How do you know? What do you know?' Fatima breathed.

'Our organisation's tendrils spread far and wide, my dear,' he said, fixing her with a look which froze her being. With that he was gone, along with her calm self assurance.

*

Fatima slept late on New Year's Day after a night of troubled sleep. She ventured out to meet Gemma in the late afternoon. Dusk was falling, most shops were closed and the streets were abnormally quiet. The ferries were running, if less frequently, and she easily found a seat inside a half empty vessel. Gemma was waiting for her at the Post Office. 'Fatima! Happy New Year,' she said, hugging her friend tightly. Fatima returned her hug, wishing she could stay safely enveloped in her arms forever. 'Where would you like to go?' enquired Gemma, releasing her.

'I think a café, if that's OK with you.'

'Yes, I don't fancy being anywhere near alcohol after last night,' Gemma admitted.

'So, it was a good party then?'

'Too good!'

They soon found a little café open in one of the side streets near the bazaar. It was a student hang-out and a few lounged around on comfy chairs and cushions, drinking cups of coffee and smoking. Gemma led her friend to a quiet corner, where there was a floor settee, covered with large, brightly coloured Turkish cushions. They ordered two coffees and settled themselves into comfortable positions.

Fatima took a sip of coffee. 'Hmm, this tastes good. So, please tell me more about this wonderful *Termal* place. I've never been there.'

Gemma's eyes became dreamy, a far-away expression on her face. 'It was like being in heaven. The air was fresh and clean and there were forests all around. I loved relaxing in the outside hot pool and I had a superb massage in the indoor bath.'

'Was there a female masseuse there?'

Gemma became flushed. 'Actually, it was one of the male attendants who gave me a massage.'

Fatima raised her eyebrows. 'Oh, I see.'

Gemma quickly changed the subject. 'You'll never guess who I met in the pool.'

'No, who?'

'Those three people who were at the restaurant when I danced.'

Fatima suddenly did not feel so good. 'You mean the ones sitting in the corner who spoke to us?'

'Yes. The Russian woman, Serkan Bey and his son, Can. They recognised me and introduced themselves, Serkan and Can, that is. The lady wasn't in the pool. Can told us later that her name's Natalia and she's a colleague of Serkan's.'

'Did you see them later?'

'Can invited Tina and I for a drink at the *Termal* Hotel's bar that evening.'

'Why did you go, Gemma?'

'Well, I was curious to find out more about them, plus Can's super dishy, is he not?'

Fatima shrugged. 'I guess he is very handsome, if you like that type.'

'So, he's not your type?'

'To be honest, Gemma, I don't know what my type is, at least not until now, anyway.'

'What do you mean, that you know now?'

'Nothing! It's not important,' Fatima said quickly.

'OK, but Can told me that he felt close to you the first time he saw you dancing.'

'Ah! Many men say they feel like this when I'm dancing: it is just their lust for my body.'

'Maybe, but I think Can does care about you. He told me to warn you that you're in danger.'

'He told you that?'

'Yes. He said that some men wanted to use you to do something illegal. He wants to protect you but he said something like he couldn't because he was too involved himself.'

Fatima shut her eyes and let out a long sigh. She twisted a strand of her hair tighter and tighter. 'Since you saw Can they have approached me, first through Mehmet Bey and then directly.'

Gemma took her hand and squeezed it. 'Please tell me what it is they want you to do, Fatima. I must help you.'

'No! You cannot help me or you'll be in danger. You must stop dancing at the restaurant and probably you should stop seeing me, although, my God, this is the last thing I want, you are such a precious friend.' Fatima began crying soundlessly, tears flowing down her cheeks.

'Here's a tissue,' Gemma said, then put her arm around her. Fatima sobbed for some time, her head buried in her friend's shoulder.

Gemma was keen to change the subject, so when Fatima's sobs had ceased she said, 'These tissues remind me that I bought them from a young woman who looked just like you.'

Fatima sat up and wiped her eyes. 'How strange! I also bought a packet from a girl who looked like my twin on the Kadıköy ferry.'

'That's so weird. I saw her at the Çamlıca ferry landing when I was out with my students. They gave me a row for buying them because the price was too high.'

'So, she gets around, this tissue seller. Actually, I gave her my card, but she has never phoned.'

'Do you think she could be your twin?'

Fatima sat silently, sipping the last of her coffee. *Should she tell her dear friend more about her past? No – she was too ashamed.* She hesitated and then said, 'Remember I told you that my mother died in childbirth?'

'Yes, of course. It's so sad.'

'Well, I think there was another girl who came after me, but I don't remember ever seeing her and no-one told me about her.'

'So what makes you believe she exists?'

'When you are a twin you just know deep within yourself that there is another.'

'I see – and this tissue seller might be her?'

'Yes, and she's the one who killed our mother.' Fatima began crying again so Gemma paid the bill and they went outside. Fatima dabbed her eyes with a tissue. 'I must catch the ferry now, Gemma. It's been lovely to see you but I am so sorry to cause you distress.'

'Not at all. I'm your friend and you can tell me anything. As I said, I want to help you. I also want to keep dancing so I'll see you next Wednesday evening at the restaurant, OK?'

'Oh, Gemma, no, it's not OK.'

'I'll be there. Everything will be all right, just you see.'

'I pray to God that you are right, Gemma.' They embraced and then Fatima hurried through the turnstile to the ferry.

TEN

Can did not sleep well and ever since he had met Fatima, his slumber was even more disturbed. He hated his situation. He had been born into crime and he was stuck with it. His beloved mother had somehow managed to extricate herself from the clutches of the Mafia several years earlier and he had no idea where she was. Every day he thought of her and now his torment had increased: that his father should wish to use the lovely Fatima in drug trafficking, just for the fun of it, was abhorrent to him. He had known many women in his twenty-eight years but the belly dancer had put a spell on him. He was besotted with her and would do anything to protect her. But how?

He was in Kadıköy on bank business when he saw a billboard advertising an English school in the main street. *Maybe that's where Gemma works*? he wondered. That was another thing he was worried about – Gemma. What would she do with the information he had given her? Would she warn Fatima that she was in danger? Had Fatima told her about the heroin and the belly dancing? What would Gemma do? The organisation had a hold over Fatima, but not Gemma. She was English. They could not easily dispose of her – it could cause an international outcry. He hardly noticed the crowds as he made his way to the Karaköy ferry terminal, so deep in thought was he. The weather was fine, but chilly, and he went to sit outside near the front of the boat, where there were no passengers. He lit a cigarette and inhaled deeply, closing his eyes. The prow plunged through the sea, gulls swooped and the *çay* sellers called. Suddenly, Can heard a sweet girl's voice. He opened his eyes to behold his darling's face. But how could this be? She was holding out a packet of tissues and wearing a headscarf with no make-up.

'Who are you?' he almost whispered.

'Who are you, sir, to ask me this?' The young woman stared defiantly at him.

Can was taken aback – he had not expected such an antagonistic response. '*Çok özür dilerim.* I am very sorry for disturbing you.'

'Thanks for your apology, sir. Why are you interested in who I am?'

'You look just like someone I know.'

'This is very interesting. I met a lady on the Üsküdar ferry who looked identical to me. She gave me her card but I have not contacted her.'

As the girl spoke Can marvelled at her voice. She spoke with a Kurdish accent like Fatima and it sounded exactly the same. If he closed his eyes he could imagine that it was his darling. The seed of an idea was taking shape in his head. 'Do you remember the name on the card?'

'Yes. It was Fatima and she is a belly dancer. I was so surprised because I can also belly dance.'

'This is too much of a coincidence! My friend is also called Fatima and she is a belly dancer,' Can said. It was Wednesday evening and he had planned to go to the restaurant to see Fatima and Gemma dancing and maybe he would have been able to speak with them. However, this chance meeting needed to be prolonged – he had to find out more about this girl.

The young woman had remained standing holding her packets of tissues, watching Can's handsome, thoughtful face closely. 'What are you thinking about, sir?'

'I am thinking that I would like to speak with you more, if that is OK?'

'If your motive is honourable I would be happy to do that,' was her careful reply.

Surely I am being honourable? He tried to convince himself. 'Let's go to a *lokanta* when the boat docks. I can buy you a meal, if you're hungry. What is your name, by the way?'

'I am always hungry, sir. My name is Fulya. What is yours?'

'Can.'

'What a beautiful name – life or soul. You are surely an admirable man.'

Admirable? Nobody has ever called me that.

*

Can found a *lokanta* in a quiet street near the Karaköy ferry terminal.

Fulya looked hungrily at the array of hot and cold dishes on offer and chose several. Can only ordered a bowl of chicken broth. There were few other customers and they sat in an alcove out of sight of the door. Can was constantly alert to the possibility that he was being watched – it affected his appetite badly. He watched Fulya attacking the food, shovelling large spoonfuls into her mouth, along with chunks of bread. She was clad in several layers of grimy clothes: a chunky grey cardigan on top, baggy Turkish trousers, thick, woollen socks and worn-looking boots on her feet. A dark, wavy strand of hair had escaped from her headscarf and her hands were red and chapped. Despite her unclean appearance, a faint, not unpleasant, musky, smoky smell, emanated from her. Once she had finished eating he ordered glasses of *çay*, in which she put several sugar lumps. 'Have you had enough to eat?' he asked.

'Yes, more than enough, Can. You are very kind.' She smiled widely at him, showing surprisingly even, white teeth.

'How do you come to be selling tissues on the ferries?' Can asked, lighting a cigarette.

'It is a way to make money.'

'Yes, but the money must be small. Are you alone here?'

'Can, I do not know why you are asking me these questions. What do you want with me?'

I must go slowly and carefully with this girl, Can thought, observing that the food and hot tea had given her cheeks a healthy colour. '*Çok özür dilerim,* Fulya. I am very sorry to upset you but I want to help you.'

'But why do you want to help me?'

Can realised that he would need to be straight with this young woman. 'Remember, I have a friend, Fatima, who looks like you? Well, I think she is in danger.'

'So, what has this got to do with me?' She glared at Can, who took a long drag of his cigarette before replying.

'Well, you could almost be twins, you look and sound so alike. Where do you come from? You have a Kurdish accent and so does she.'

'Well, I cannot hide my accent. I come from a small mountain village in the east, near the Iraqi border. But how is this important?'

'Do you have a family, Fulya? What made you leave your home?'

'You have not answered my question, Can, but I can say that I'm an orphan. My mother died in childbirth. I was sent away to live with some distant relatives in Diyarbakır.'

'Oh, the capital of Kurdistan? You must have seen a lot of conflict?'

'Indeed, it was a dangerous place. This is why I came to Istanbul.' Fulya fiddled with a strand of hair, trying to put it back under her headscarf.

'And you came here all alone?'

'Yes!' she said defiantly.

There's more to this tale, Can decided. 'So, I know something of Fatima's background. It is similar to yours and I think it's very likely that you are twins.'

'That may be, but again I ask you, how is this important?'

'I told you that Fatima's in danger. If you look identical and can belly dance as well as her, you could impersonate her.'

'Then I'd be in danger!'

'I cannot deny that this is true, but I have some influence. Your lifestyle would improve enormously. You'd have a comfortable place to live and plenty of money.' Can looked earnestly at her, trying not to show how nervous he was.

'This sounds like a fairy tale. May I ask what your business is?'

'I work for an international organisation which deals in finance.'

'I am not stupid! What you say is extremely vague. If she is in danger there must be something criminal happening.'

Can looked carefully around the *lokanta* and lowered his voice. 'The organisation is involved in the drug trade. The top men want to mix business with pleasure. They love to watch beautiful women belly dance and when they saw Fatima they began to fantasise that they were stuffing her bodice with drugs instead of money.'

Fulya laughed loudly. 'This is a big joke! The drugs would surely be too heavy for her clothes.'

'This, unfortunately could be part of their fun as her clothes may slip off. That could lead to unpleasant developments.'

'Unpleasant indeed, but what does she do with the drugs?'

'She will pass them on to Mehmet Bey, the restaurant owner and he will give them to other traffickers who will take them out of the country to Europe.'

'It sounds fantastical!' Fulya's eyes sparkled with excitement.

'Yes, I suppose it is but are you interested in doing this?'

'Possibly, if I can do some dealing.'

Can regarded her with interest. 'Do you know anything about this?'

'Yes, indeed I do. I've sold more than packets of tissues and I have lots of contacts,' she boasted.

Can's brain worked hard, trying to reassess the situation. He had thought Fulya was a homeless, poor orphan, who scraped a living simply selling tissues. 'I'll have to see what can be done about that,' he said carefully.

'Good, I hope we can do business together.'

*

Can excused himself and went to the toilet where he came to a decision. He returned to Fulya who was sitting at the table, a faraway look on her face. 'Well, Fulya, how would you like to accompany me to my residence? You'll have your own room and I won't expect anything from you, except that tomorrow I'll buy you some better clothes. I need to see your figure and also your dancing, then we can make a plan.'

'What poor girl could refuse such an offer. My bedroom is a small cave in a park. I have an old mattress and some blankets stored there and I share it with some other women. We make a fire on cold evenings, share our food and life experiences. It's fun in good weather, but not now in winter.'

'Will they be worried about you if you don't turn up?'

'Only for a short time. People come and go. When you're homeless you never know what each day will bring. Look at me today!'

'Good. Let's go now,' Can said. They walked to a nearby car park where an attendant was watching the cars. Can gave him some money and led Fulya to his vehicle – a big, black Mercedes.

'*Maşallah*! Is this your car?' Fulya gasped as Can held the front passenger door open. She slid into the soft seat, the smell of leather engulfing her.

Can drove through the evening traffic in silence with Fulya dozing beside him. He went along the road beside the Bosphorus, under the first bridge and towards the second one. Fulya woke up. 'Where are you taking me, Can? We are far up the Bosphorus.'

'Don't worry, we'll be there soon.' A few minutes later he slowed down and took a right turn along a track to the sea, where he parked the car. A yacht with two masts was anchored a short distance from the shore.

'Where is your home, Can?' said Fulya, looking around anxiously.

'Right there,' Can replied, pointing to the yacht.

'You're not serious! If I go there I'll be a prisoner, unless I swim ashore.'

'Can you swim?' Can chuckled at the thought of her trying to swim with all her heavy clothes.

'Of course! Can you?'

'I am an excellent swimmer, but don't worry, there's a dinghy.' He got out of the car and she followed hesitantly. Hidden underneath some bushes was the dinghy. He pulled it out and began to drag it towards the sea. Once there he ordered Fulya to get in.

She stood with her arms crossed. It was a cloudy night and Can could not make out her face, but her voice was filled with fear. 'If I go with you to that boat I'll be completely at your mercy.'

'You are right, Fulya, but I have already told you that I am an honourable man. There is no-one else on the yacht and actually we are safer there.'

'Are you in danger too?'

'Yes, I am, especially now I have you with me.'

'OK, I'll go with you because if I stay here it will be cold and uncomfortable.'

'That's right. On my yacht you'll have your own cabin and there's a shower.'

'A shower! This is making me want to go even more.'

With that Can held her hand and helped her into the dinghy. He took the oars from the bottom of it and began rowing strongly towards the yacht. The sea was calm, only a slight breeze ruffling the surface. In the distance moving lights from huge cargo ships lit up the water. A few gulls shrieked and somewhere a dog barked. The sea smelled of sewage and oily, rotting seaweed near the shore but further out the air became fresher and cleaner. As they neared the yacht Fulya asked, 'How do we get on board?'

'There is a ladder down the side. I hope you are a good climber.'

'I'm like a monkey,' she giggled.

Can steadied the dinghy while she stood on the first rung of the steel ladder and quickly climbed up. 'Just like a monkey!' he shouted. Fulya's laughter hung on the breeze as he hoisted himself onto the deck. When they had both stopped laughing Can gave her a tour. 'This wooden yacht is called a *gulet* and is made in Turkey,' he began.

Fulya looked around, taking in the polished dark wood of the deck, the beautifully carved doors and window frames. 'It is a wonderful *gulet*.'

'It is indeed – wait until you see the interior,' Can replied, unlocking and opening the door. Fulya gasped when she saw the luxurious saloon: comfortable-looking sofas with huge scatter cushions lined one wall, a long coffee table with a fruit bowl in front of them, a magnificent wooden table with six dining chairs another. A wall-mounted television was opposite the settees, a stereo system on a shelf beneath it. The floor was polished wood, with a wooden pillar in the centre and smaller pillars between the windows. Adjacent to the saloon was a well-equipped galley kitchen. The shower room and toilet plus three cabins were accessed from a short hallway. Everywhere smelt of newly varnished wood and Fulya stood entranced, breathing it in deeply. Can opened the door of a cabin. 'This is your room, Fulya.' She gaped in amazement at the double bed, clean bedding and pillows piled upon it, the soft woollen carpet, the wardrobe and dressing table with chair, the bedside lights on fitted tables underneath the windows, at which hung frilly cream curtains. The ceiling had curved, smooth wooden beams which glowed in the lamp light.

'I have never lived anywhere as wonderful,' Fulya said in amazement.

Can opened the wardrobe. 'You may use this dressing gown and there's a nightdress and some casual clothes.'

'It's as if you were expecting me,' Fulya said, fingering the towelling robe's fluffiness.

'This is the guest room and I like to keep everything my guests might need. There's a shower outside where you'll find shower gel and shampoo.'

'May I have one now?'

'Of course. If you require anything else, please tell me. Tomorrow I shall go and buy you some more clothes and a belly dance costume. Are you happy to stay here?'

'Can't I go with you?'

'I'd rather you stayed here out of sight for now. There's food in the kitchen – just help yourself.'

'So, no standing on the deck shouting, "help!"'

'Please say you are joking, Fulya.'

'Naturally I'm joking – you need to lighten up.'

'Sorry, it's getting late and I'm feeling stressed. I'm going to have a drink and then go to bed, is that all right?'

'Yes. Will I see you in the morning?'

'That depends what time you wake up. I'm planning to leave quite early so you might as well have a good rest.'

'OK, good night and thank you Can.'

'*Iyi geceler*, Fulya. I'll see you some time tomorrow.'

Fulya's slumber was deep and long; Can's was troubled, his mind revolving pointlessly as he thought about the twins.

*

A thick fog surrounded the boat when Can left in the morning. He strained his eyes, trying to see the shore and his car. A slight breeze blew some fog away and he was able to locate the landing place. He closely examined his car to see if it had been tampered with. Everything seemed normal so he got in and began driving back along the track and then the road towards the centre of Istanbul. At the first shopping mall he stopped and bought some food and wine. He chose some more casual clothes for Fulya, as well as a thick, waterproof coat. Next he visited a shop selling belly dance outfits. He spent a long time looking and found a turquoise costume which was similar to the one Fatima had been wearing when he first met her.

It was nearly noon by the time he had finished so he drove back to the boat through traffic-clogged streets. He quickly loaded up the dinghy with his purchases and rowed towards the yacht. A hazy sun had caused the fog to lift, giving the air a welcome warmth. Fulya had seen him coming and came to the top of the ladder to greet him and help with the bags. '*Hoş geldin,* Can. You have bought a lot of things.'

'Yes, and they're all for you. Are you hungry? I've brought some lunch,' he said carrying the bags inside.

'Yes, I'm ravenous – I think it's the sea air.' Can took in her changed appearance: gone was the headscarf, her long, glossy black hair tumbling around her shoulders. She was dressed in a pair of black jogging trousers, a T-shirt and maroon fleece on top. Can was amazed at her likeness to Fatima – even her hair was the same length, the same waviness and the same glossiness. Her clothes, while still loose-fitting, revealed a slim figure and he could hardly wait to see her in the belly dance outfit. But first they must eat, his stomach warned him, as he at last felt hungry.

At the rear of the yacht, underneath a canopy, was a large table and some chairs. 'Shall we eat outside?' Fulya enquired.

'Yes, I think it's warm enough.' Fulya busied herself with laying the table while Can unpacked the bags of food. He observed the contented look on his guest's face and hoped that it would stay like that. He poured two half glasses of red wine and offered her one, not wishing to get her drunk.

'Oh, thanks Can,' she said, taking a glass. 'It's been ages since I've tasted wine.' They sat down to eat, wishing each other, '*afiyet olsun.*' They ate mainly in silence, concentrating on the food, occasionally pausing to gaze at the variety of shipping passing by in the middle of the strait, the Asian shore's hills and houses a scenic backdrop. Fulya cleared her plate and drained her glass with obvious pleasure.

'Anything else to eat? Some more wine?'

'I do not wish to appear greedy, Can, but I would like both.'

Can poured her a full glass of wine and spooned more food onto her plate, saying, 'There's plenty – eat as much as you like. I think you are slimmer than Fatima, so you need to put on a few kilos.'

'It's not surprising that I am skinny. I've been semi-starved ever since I came to Istanbul,' Fulya said, slipping an olive into her mouth.

Can lit a cigarette and looked thoughtfully at her. 'How long have you been here?'

'I arrived in the heat of summer, so it must be about 18 months, I think.'

'And you've been hard up all that time? What about when you were selling drugs?'

Fulya shifted in her seat, frowning slightly. 'Since you ask, I never made much money. I was either ripped off or robbed.'

'That's too bad.'

'I hope that this does not happen to me again,' Fulya said, giving her host a meaningful stare.

'I'll do my best to prevent it,' he promised, continuing, 'could you try on the belly dance outfit now, Fulya?'

'I would prefer to have a rest first, then I can wear it.'

'OK, I'm looking forward to it,' Can said, with the ghost of a smile.

While Fulya rested he cleared the table, then sat smoking, staring out to sea, feeling strangely calm. He must have dozed off, for suddenly he became aware of a presence beside him, accompanied by a sweet-smelling perfume. Fulya stood, wearing her costume, smiling at him. She had made up her face and had brushed her hair until it shone. Can shook his head in disbelief – *was he dreaming*? What he saw was a slightly slimmer version of Fatima: it was uncanny. 'How do I look, Can?'

'Incredible! You look exactly like Fatima, just a bit slimmer.'

'This is good. I will keep eating a lot – that is no hardship.'

'Would it be possible to show me your dancing?' he dared to ask.

'Certainly, if you have some music.'

Can disappeared into the lounge and soon the sound of music could be heard. Fulya followed him inside and began to raise her arms, fixing her host with a smouldering look. He sat on the settee watching intently as she showed him her moves. Her breasts were as big and shapely as Fatima's but her belly and bottom needed more fat to fill out her curves. She danced for a while longer, then stopped, giving him a small bow. 'So, how do I compare with her?'

'Your sister. . .'

'Please do not call her my sister,' Fulya begged.

'Why ever not?'

'Because I do not want to remember my family. It is too painful.' She sat down beside Can, her hands clasped tightly.

'OK, OK. Your dancing is good but Fatima is more fluid and performs more moves.'

'Would the men notice this?'

'I'm not sure but their leader, Serkan Bey, certainly would,' Can said, knowing his father's obsession with detail.

'This Serkan Bey sounds like a problem. What can we do about it?'

Can knew what needed to be done, but he was reluctant to suggest it. 'I'm afraid that Fatima will have to teach you her moves,' he said, lighting another cigarette and taking a long drag.

'No! I don't want this. Surely there's another way?' Fulya exploded, frantically twisting a strand of her hair.

'I don't want this either, Fulya but I think it's the only way. I was hoping that we could make this swap without Fatima's knowledge, but to be honest I can't see how this could be done.' He gave a deep sigh and poured himself a whisky from a cut glass decanter on the coffee table.

ELEVEN

At the same time Can and Fulya were having dinner in the Karaköy *lokanta*, Gemma was nearby hurrying towards the Tünel on her way to the restaurant where Fatima was anxiously waiting. She desperately wanted to see Gemma but simultaneously hoped that she would change her mind and not come to dance. Each morning since her brief encounter with Serkan Bey she had awoken with a feeling of dread and each night before she drifted off to sleep she gave thanks to God for another safe day.

Mehmet Bey had been avoiding her since New Year's Eve but that evening he knocked on her door as she was making up her face. 'Come in,' she called.

'I'm sorry to disturb you, Fatima, but I was wondering if Gemma was coming this evening?' Fatima noticed that her boss was not in his usual well-groomed state: he was unshaven, his hair untidy and his clothes crumpled.

'I'm not sure. I last saw her New Year's Day and she said she was coming then.'

Mehmet shook his head from side to side, tutted and frowned. 'To be honest, Fatima, I was hoping that she wouldn't come. Her presence here now presents us with a problem, I am sure you understand.'

'Yes, I do but she really enjoyed dancing in front of an audience.'

'Hmm, yes I saw that but what if she should be here when this business with drugs starts? You haven't told her anything, have you?'

'No, of course not,' Fatima said, hoping that her boss would not detect the lie, and anyway, she had not given her any details. It was Can's fault for warning Gemma that she was in danger.

'Well, we'll just have to hope that Serkan Bey gives us warning, and then you can make up something to stop her coming that night.'

He doesn't seem to have thought this through at all, Fatima thought. 'Surely Serkan has to give you sufficient warning because you would need to close the restaurant that night.'

'Right, yes. Unless they're mad enough to do it in the midst of a normal night – it might give them an extra kick to fool the tourists and ordinary Turks.'

'What an incredible idea!' Fatima's half made-up eyes widened in disbelief.

They both jumped at a knock on the door. 'It's Gemma,' came her voice and Mehmet held a finger to his lips before he let her in. '*Iyi geceler,* Mehmet Bey,' Gemma said, then gave Fatima a kiss on both cheeks.

'Do I not get the same treatment?' her boss wanted to know, so she reluctantly kissed his cheeks, his stubble pricking her lips. With that he left the room, urging them to hurry up and get ready.

*

Once Fatima was certain he had gone she looked at Gemma with despair and said in a low voice, 'Why did you come? I don't want you to be here.'

'I told you I would come, Fatima. I'm your friend and I'll protect you, although I'm still not clear what I'm going to protect you from.'

'Never mind, there's not time to discuss this now – we need to get ready.' Fatima turned back to her mirror and applied more mascara.

'OK,' said Gemma, 'but you are going to have to tell me more.'

'Why don't you stay with me again tonight, then we can talk about it in the morning.'

Gemma reluctantly agreed, the memory of her uncomfortable night on Fatima's settee still fresh in her mind.

The restaurant was packed once again, with no sign of the Mafia, much to Fatima's relief. She danced alone, then together with Gemma, both receiving uproarious applause and many tips. At the end of the evening Mehmet Bey congratulated them, commenting, 'With both of you dancing you are receiving more than double tips.'

'That's great,' Gemma enthused, adding, 'so I'll be able to dance every Wednesday now.'

Her boss saw Fatima's concerned expression but nevertheless replied, 'Yes, Gemma, I think this is possible.'

Gemma excused herself and went to the bathroom. While she was away Fatima vented her frustration. 'Why did you say that she could dance here every Wednesday after what you told me before?' she hissed.

Mehmet held out his hands despairingly. 'What could I say, Fatima? I cannot tell her anything and she is good for business.'

'That's all you think about – money and your wretched business,' Fatima shrieked, as Gemma returned, looking hesitantly around the door.

'I hope I'm not interrupting anything,' she said, noticing how upset her friend was.

'No, no, nothing at all,' her boss said soothingly. 'I'll call you girls a taxi. It's getting late. Are you staying with Fatima again?' he asked Gemma.

'Yes, I am.'

'That's good – it's better than going home alone,' he said to Gemma, at the same time giving Fatima a penetrating look.

Let him look at me all he wants, she thought. *He can't stop me telling my dear friend anything.*

*

When they reached Fatima's flat, she said, 'I could do with a drink. Would you like some wine, Gemma?'

'Yes, I think we need it after our exertions.'

'Also after what I had to put up with from my boss,' Fatima said, joining Gemma on the settee and pouring them large glasses of red wine.

'It sounded as if you were having an argument.'

'Yes, we were, but let's not talk about it now – I want to relax.' She took Gemma's hand in hers and squeezed it tightly. 'Are you OK with sleeping on my sofa again, Gemma?'

'Well, I guess I am but it's not very comfortable,' her friend admitted, adding, 'but there's nowhere else to sleep, is there?'

Fatima took a sip of wine and gazed deep into Gemma's eyes. 'You could sleep with me in my comfy double bed.'

Gemma returned Fatima's gaze, wondering what it meant. 'I suppose that would be better, if you don't mind,' she said carefully.

'You are being so polite, so English,' Fatima laughed. 'Naturally, I don't mind.' She went into her bedroom, leaving the door open and lay in bed, listening to Gemma brushing her teeth in the bathroom.

She hugged herself under the quilt, trying to heat up the bed, then curled her legs up under her fleecy nightie. Gemma came in, wearing a long T-shirt and pants and slid into bed, shivering slightly. 'You're cold, aren't you? The *kalorifer* has gone off for the night. Snuggle into me to get warm.' Fatima was lying on her side and Gemma turned towards her back, pressing her body into the nightgown's fleeciness, smelling her friend's muskiness. She gingerly stroked Fatima's hair, marvelling at its silky softness. After some minutes Fatima turned over and enveloped Gemma in her arms. They lay entwined, feeling the heat of their bodies mingling, breathing in each other's scent. Fatima ran her fingers through Gemma's short, wavy hair, then traced the outline of her friend's lips with her forefinger. 'What are you thinking?' she asked.

Gemma smiled. 'I am not thinking anything. I am simply enjoying being here with you and feeling warm.'

'Have you ever been close like this to a woman before?'

'No, I never have.'

'Me neither. In fact I've had little experience with men since I left my home village – that was enough,' she said with a shudder.

'Do you want to tell me about it?' Gemma asked, trying to see into Fatima's fathomless dark eyes in the soft lamp light.

'No, not now. Let's not spoil this moment.' Fatima began slowly moving her hands up and down Gemma's body, feeling her curves, her softness, the beating of her heart. Then she moved towards Gemma's mouth and began to kiss her, gently at first, then, as she felt her friend responding, more urgently. Soon they were writhing together, the intensity of their emotions driving them into ecstasy. Slowly they came down from their high and breathlessly stared at each other in surprise.

'Oh, Fatima – what happened to us?' Gemma whispered into Fatima's ear.

'I don't know, Gemma, but it was beautiful, wasn't it?'

'Hmm, yes, very,' Gemma sighed. They fell asleep, still entwined, only waking in the grey light of morning.

*

Fatima carefully extricated herself from Gemma's embrace and went to the bathroom. She looked at her face in the mirror: it seemed different, softer somehow, her frown lines fainter, her mouth relaxed, her eyes aglow. She smiled at herself and silently prayed, 'thank you.' She padded barefoot into the kitchen and made two cups of coffee which she took to the bedroom, carefully placing one on the table next to Gemma, the other on the one beside her. Gemma stirred slightly, then stretched.

'Is that coffee I smell?' she asked, her eyes still shut.

'*Evet, canım.* Yes, my darling.'

Gemma sleepily opened her eyes, saw her friend, then rubbed them hard. 'I had such a strange dream, or maybe it wasn't a dream?' She sat up and began to sip her coffee.

'I don't know, but if it was the same dream that I had, then it was very beautiful.' They smiled knowingly at each other, reluctant to break the spell.

'I must go soon,' Gemma said, breaking it.

'Must you? We're both free today, we could spend it together.'

'I'd love to do that but Tina will be worrying about me and I've got lessons to prepare and piles of homework to mark.'

Is she making up excuses to leave me? Fatima's paranoia was taking over. 'Please stay and have some breakfast, plus I need to tell you more about what's happening.'

Gemma looked at her friend's worried face. Only a few moments before she had seemed so relaxed. 'OK, I'll stay for breakfast,' she relented.

'Good,' Fatima said, then got up and put on her dressing gown.

'May I help you?'

'No, I would like to prepare it for you. Please have a shower, if you want.'

Gemma appeared in the kitchen, fully dressed and smelling of her friend's lavender soap. She sat down at the table which was laid out with Turkish breakfast fayre – bread, butter, black olives, white goat's cheese, honey, boiled eggs, sliced tomatoes and cucumber. A big pot of *çay* stood on a mat in the centre, along with two tulip-shaped tea glasses and a bowl of sugar. Fatima bent to kiss her forehead. 'You smell divine,' she breathed into Gemma's hair.

'*Teşekkür ederim.* Thank you for this lovely breakfast.' They ate in companionable silence, each lost in their own thoughts and not quite sure what to say to each other. Fatima, though, felt compelled to tell Gemma more and to repeat her warning of the danger. Once they were finished eating she began.

'So, Gemma, you remember that Can warned you I was in danger because the Mafia want me to become involved in something illegal?'

'Yes, that's right, but neither of you have told me what that might be.'

'I know. It's because we want to protect you – the more you know the more dangerous it could be for you.'

'But I want to protect you, so I must know more,' Gemma insisted.

'I do not want you to become involved but I will tell you what I know because you are most dear to me. The Mafia men want me to belly dance for them and instead of placing notes in my costume, they will put small packets of drugs, mainly heroin.'

'What? Why do they want to do this?' Gemma laughed out loud in amazement.

'I know it sounds fantastic. Mehmet Bey told me that they want some fun. They love my dancing and they want to combine it with their trafficking.'

'But surely you can just refuse to do it?'

'I wish I could, but I can't. Serkan Bey, who's the leader, came into my dressing room and told me that they know why I left my homeland and came here. If I refuse to do what they want they will tell my boss and everyone else in the neighbourhood. My job would be gone, my flat, everything. I would be ruined.'

She began to sob and Gemma put her arms around her and let her cry and cry. Once her sobs had finished she asked, 'Was it so bad, what happened?'

Fatima sat up straight and quietly said, 'I told you that after my mother died I was raised by my father's youngest sister. My aunt was kind and sent me to school, where I learned some English. She wasn't the problem. It was my uncle, her husband. He was an animal. When she was out visiting relatives or working and we were alone in the house, he did vile things to me. I shall never forget it. It made me feel unclean. That's why I don't ever want to be touched by a man again. That's why I ran away to Istanbul.'

'Oh, Fatima, that's terrible. I am so sorry for you.'

'Gemma, please, do not feel sorry for me. I have an inner strength which God gives me and with His help I can overcome anything.'

'That's good that you have that faith, Fatima. I'm not sure about God but it must be wonderful to believe.'

'It is wonderful, Gemma. I visit a saint's tomb in Üsküdar. One day maybe we can go there together and you'll find peace,' Fatima said, clasping her friend's hand.

'I'd like to do that, Fatima, but now I really must go. I'll see you at the restaurant next Wednesday and if anything happens before that, please ring me.'

'Of course, dear Gemma, and please take care,' Fatima said as she accompanied her to the door and gave her a quick hug. She went to the lounge window and watched her walk rapidly away, without a backward glance. She sank down on her sofa, suddenly overwhelmed with sadness. Her love for Gemma was huge, but did she feel the same? She doubted it.

TWELVE

Gemma was forced to sit inside on the Kadıköy ferry. The weather was cold and wet with a strong wind blowing off the sea. The interior of the boat was stiflingly hot, a pungent smell of damp clothes filling the air. The passengers sat forlornly staring into space, or buried in a newspaper. They only came to life to order *çay* or to listen to the sellers of various implements who were demonstrating their usefulness. Gemma closed her eyes, trying to stop her mind from remembering Fatima's kisses and embraces. She was in a state of shock – surely she wasn't a lesbian? She had never felt attracted to women; even at school she had never had a crush on a female teacher. She liked men too much and thought longingly of the lovely Can. He would find it difficult to have a relationship with Fatima if she were a lesbian. But maybe she had simply been put off because of her uncle? If she were able to overcome her revulsion with a man as gorgeous as Can, he might have a chance. However, he was in the Mafia, his father was their leader, so Fatima should not become involved with him. Gemma's thoughts shifted into wondering how she could help her friend – surely there must be a way?

By the time the ferry had docked, Gemma had decided to accept her ex-student Hasan's offer of a date. He was the one who had told her and Tina about the *Termal*. He had come to their New Year's Eve party. They had danced together and at midnight he had kissed her. He was only a couple of years younger than her, was easy to talk to and quite handsome, although not like Can, she thought wistfully.

Tina was busy preparing lessons when Gemma arrived home. She left her umbrella open in the hall and hung her raincoat over the back of a chair to dry. 'It's foul out,' she told Tina.

'Yes, I can see that. I'm not budging out of here today. So, where have you been? At the belly dancer's, I guess?'

'Yes, that's right,' said Gemma, trying unsuccessfully not to blush. Luckily her flatmate was not looking at her, her attention still focussed on her books.

'Would you like a cuppa?' Gemma asked, heading towards the kitchen.

'Yes, that would be great. Any excuse to stop working.'

Gemma came back carrying two steaming mugs. She told Tina about her dancing but not about the drugs and definitely not about her time in Fatima's bed. *That would be too embarrassing*! Instead she announced, 'I'm going to go on a date with Hasan. He asked me at New Year and I've been thinking about it.'

'Great! Hasan seems like a good guy and you're not teaching him any more, not that it's against the law or anything, but I guess it could be a bit tricky teaching a guy that you were having a scene with.'

'Yes, right. I know some teachers who've done that and it hasn't worked out too well.'

'Yeah! There was that one, Adnan I think his name was. He thought that by going out with his teacher she'd give him top marks. She didn't and he went and complained about her.'

'Yes, ghastly. Well, there's no chance of that happening with Hasan. He's at advanced level and I'm not teaching that yet.'

'Well, good luck with it. I'd better get back to my prep.,' Tina said.

*

When the following Wednesday arrived, Gemma had already had two dates with Hasan. On the first meeting they had gone to the cinema, then to a café for coffee and cake. The second time they went out to dinner at a restaurant near Gemma's flat. Afterwards she had invited him back for a drink. They ended up in bed and he stayed the night. Gemma had enjoyed the experience but she could not help comparing it with how she'd felt with Fatima – it wasn't the same. The intensity, the passion, the feeling of oneness was missing. *Was she a lesbian*? She did not think so, but she had to admit that she was attracted to Fatima. She wanted to see her very much but nevertheless she phoned and told her she had a bad cold. Half of Istanbul seemed to be suffering with wintry coughs and sneezes, so this was an easy lie to tell. Fatima seemed to accept it, wishing her, *'geçmiş olsun,'* may it soon pass.

Gemma was fascinated by Turkish culture and had asked Hasan

many questions about it, so she should not have been surprised to receive an invitation to his nephew Ibrahim's circumcision party. *Why would anyone wish to celebrate such a private thing as having their son's foreskin cut?* she thought, but did not ask Hasan. Out loud she enthusiastically accepted the invite, which was on the following Saturday afternoon. She wondered what she should wear and Hasan said, 'You don't need to dress up – just come in your usual clothes.' Gemma did not feel reassured and decided to wear a smart woollen skirt and jumper, with black tights and her knee-length leather boots. The party was to be held inside but she did not know whether the place would be sufficiently heated.

When Hasan came to meet her he explained that they would be going in his car, which he had parked at the edge of the bazaar. They crawled through the Saturday traffic until they reached his nephew's home, which was not far away from Gemma's flat. A crowd of people were gathered outside the apartment, all chatting animatedly and admiring the six-year-old, who was wearing his circumcision party costume. He looked like a little Ottoman sultan in his sparkling white outfit, a glittery crown upon his head, topped with a white feather, a cape falling down his back, trousers with a golden embroidered waistband and a long-sleeved shirt with gold embroidery down the front and a bow tie. On his feet were white shoes and socks.

Several of Hasan's relatives greeted Gemma in Turkish, but before she could get sucked in to the greetings ritual Hasan announced that they all would drive around in their cars, following the young sultan and showing him off to the neighbourhood. Gemma squeezed in to the back of Hasan's car, squashed between two plump ladies with an old man sitting in the front seat. 'This is Ibrahim's grandfather and the ladies beside you are two of his aunts,' Hasan told Gemma as he began to follow the lead car, the child sitting proudly erect in the front, waving regally to passers-by, who waved back. There was a football match at the nearby Fenerbahçe stadium, which increased the volume of vehicles, the crowd's noise adding to the traffic's din. Eventually they reached the coastal road and increased their speed, the Sea of Marmara and its islands a scenic distraction for Gemma, who was feeling frustrated and uncomfortable. She could not see the sense of the expedition and only later understood the importance of this ritual: it was a boy's first rite of passage into manhood and the more people that knew about it, the better.

After some time the cavalcade turned round and went back, meeting crowds of football supporters streaming out of the stadium. 'It looks like Fenerbahçe has won,' said Gemma, observing the masses who were singing and waving yellow and blue flags.

'Yes, they like to make as much noise as possible,' Can replied as cars full of supporters drove by, hooting loudly and driving dangerously. Finally they arrived at the party venue, a large hall near the boy's house. It was packed with guests, the old folks sitting, the women mostly wearing headscarves, while their husbands smoked. Younger people were milling around chatting and laughing while others congregated at the edges where long tables were piled high with sandwiches and other finger food, bottles of juice and water and paper cups and plates.

Gemma headed for the food – she was starving after the long drive, but she had just bitten into a sandwich when Hasan appeared. 'They're about to perform the operation,' he told her, beckoning her to follow him, which she did reluctantly. Ibrahim was lying on a table covered in red velvet in the centre of the room, surrounded by his nervous, adoring family. Two official-looking men were near him, one wearing a white coat. 'That's the doctor,' murmured Hasan, to Gemma's relief. She had been imagining an unskilled man wielding a sharp knife doing the deed. The doctor rubbed iodine-soaked cotton wool around the boy's genitals and then Gemma averted her eyes as he cut the foreskin, the lad's cry of pain piercing her like a knife. The other man was a religious leader who recited verses from the Qur'an during the procedure.

Afterwards Ibrahim was fussed over and given sweets and other gifts. Then he was whisked onto the dance floor where he dutifully allowed his many relatives to jig around with him. Gemma watched him sympathetically. 'Surely he's in a lot of pain,' she said to Hasan.

'No, I don't think so, Gemma. The doctor gave him a local anaesthetic and he's feeling happy with all his presents and the attention he's getting. This is how I remember mine, although maybe I have forgotten the pain.' Gemma hoped that what Hasan had said was true and allowed him to lead her to the dance floor where belly dance music was playing. He was quite good at it, holding his arms out straight and clicking his fingers as he moved deftly around her.

She was beginning to enjoy herself, her movements becoming more fluid as she relaxed. Hasan looked at her admiringly, as did several of the other dancers, who began to stand back and clap in approval. Gemma's innate desire to be in the limelight made her dancing more complex as she remembered what Fatima had taught her. It was the first time that Hasan had seen her perform and afterwards he asked her where she had learned how to dance.

'I studied belly dance a bit in England,' she told him.

'But your movements are so good, Gemma. I think you have had lessons here from an exceptional dancer,' he persisted.

Gemma found herself, despite her misgivings, telling him about her first visit to the restaurant, about Fatima's teachings and about her two performances. She did not mention the Mafia connection or her relationship with Fatima. 'You are, what do you say in English? A dark horse? I must come and see your next show.'

'Oh, no! Please don't come, Hasan. I'd be far too embarrassed.'

'Nonsense! You weren't at all embarrassed just now. What are you afraid of?'

What can I do? He is getting too suspicious, Gemma thought and heard herself agreeing for him to accompany her the following Wednesday evening. *Maybe it's better if Fatima sees me with Hasan,* she decided, although she was not convinced.

THIRTEEN

Can sat sipping his whisky, its warm glow relaxing him as he watched Fulya sitting resplendent in her belly dance costume. He could not understand her reluctance at meeting Fatima. As an only child he would have given anything to have discovered a long lost sibling. Fulya had been thinking hard about how she could learn Fatima's dance moves without having to actually meet her. 'How about you making a video of her dancing?' she suggested.

Can raised his eyebrows at this idea – if he had a video of his darling he'd watch it constantly. 'This is a great idea, Fulya, but I can't see Fatima agreeing to it.'

'But if you have such power over her, how can she refuse?'

If only I did have power over her! It was his father who had the power, a fact which now was frustrating him intensely. 'Unfortunately it's Serkan Bey who has the power, not me.'

'Well, couldn't he get her to agree to be videoed?'

Can drained his whisky and poured another, along with a glass of wine for Fulya. 'Neither Serkan Bey nor any of the other Mafia must know about this swap – surely you can understand that?'

'Oh, right. That's why I have to be able to dance as well as Fatima, and also become as plump as her. Sorry, Can. I'm getting tired and have drunk a little too much wine.'

'That's all right, Fulya. We also don't want Mehmet Bey to know about this, or indeed anyone else. That's another reason why we need to tell Fatima, because she'll tell us the time and place where the drugs will be traded.'

'That's if they tell her beforehand – they might just drive her to a secret location.'

Can ran his fingers through his thick black hair and sighed. 'We have to hope that this doesn't happen. The best scenario will be if they use the usual restaurant.'

Fulya tried to stifle a yawn. 'I want to sleep now, Can. I suppose I must agree to meeting her.'

Can smiled at her. 'You may live to thank me for reuniting you with your twin sister.'

'Reuniting? We were only together in the womb,' Fulya cried, her eyes flashing anger. 'Good night, Can. I'll see you in the morning,' she said as she left the saloon.

'*Iyi geceler,*' he called after her.

*

Fulya was up before Can in the morning and busied herself preparing the breakfast table on the outside deck. It was an unusually fine day for January, a hazy sun shining through the morning fog onto the sea, the swell from distant cargo ships making the yacht heave slightly. Can slept late and appeared bleary-eyed and unshaven, the stale smell of whisky on his breath. 'Thanks for making breakfast, Fulya,' he said, rubbing his stubbly chin.

'*Günaydın,* Can. How are you this fine morning?'

Despite his throbbing head Can could not help feeling his heart lift at the sight of Fulya, her eyes shining, a welcoming smile on her face. 'Good morning, Fulya. I drank too much whisky last night but the wine does not seem to have affected you.'

'No, I feel fine. Would you like some tea or coffee?'

'A coffee would be great,' Can said, catching a whiff of lemon cologne as Fulya bent near him to fill his cup. She also passed him a bottle of water, without comment.

I could get used to being waited on like this by a beautiful woman, Can mused, and then rebuked himself as he remembered Fatima. He took several sips of coffee and drank a glass of water before speaking. 'Thanks for saying you'd see Fatima last night. I'm going to phone her at the restaurant today and, if God wills, she'll agree to meet me.'

'Will you tell her about me when you phone?'

'No. I'll wait until we meet. I'll tell her that it's very important.'

'OK, and if she agrees to meet me, will you bring her here?'

'No, because I don't think she would come, at least not at first. She hardly knows me and probably doesn't trust me,' Can said, realising that he actually knew Fulya better than her twin already.

'That's true. I certainly didn't trust you, but then I did not have much to lose,' Fulya said with a grin.

'Well, I hope you trust me now.' He looked at Fulya intently, trying to read her thoughts.

'I'm beginning to after two safe nights, Can.'

'Good. Assuming that she will meet you I guess it'll have to be in a café because the weather is too unpredictable to meet outside. I've been thinking about this and I'm going to have to ask you to wear the niqab and chador.'

'What! You want me to wear a face veil which only shows my eyes and a black body cloak, like a devout Muslim?'

'That's right. I cannot risk being seen with the two of you. This is the only way to do it.'

He was saddened to observe that Fulya's morning happiness had evaporated. She sat staring sulkily at him. Suddenly she brightened. 'I have a better idea – Fatima covers up instead.'

Once again Can was impressed by this young woman's candidness. 'I shall ask her but I can't promise that she will do it.'

'Great! You can surely charm her into doing anything, Can,'

How I wish this were true, he thought.

*

There was no phone on the yacht so Can had to go to the nearest post office to contact Fatima. He went in the early evening when she would be preparing for her performance, leaving Fulya alone on the boat. She did not seem to mind. There was plenty to entertain her with the television, stereo and books to read, indeed she was content to stay there for a while after her hard life on the streets.

Mehmet Bey answered the phone and when he heard it was Can he immediately called Fatima. 'Hello, Fatima,' Can said in response to her subdued 'hello.' They then went through the polite Turkish greetings and having ascertained that both were well, Can told her that he wanted to meet her.

'Why do you want to see me?' she asked, sounding as feisty as her sister.

'I cannot explain over the phone but it is important,' Can said, in what he hoped was a commanding voice.

'All right,' she said.

Can wished that she sounded more amenable and remembered how she had turned away from his kiss at New Year. He tried to make his voice sound compassionate when he suggested meeting at the ancient *Yerebatan Sarnıcı*, the Basilica Cistern, in the Sultanahmet part of Istanbul. It was his favourite place and he hoped that the Mafia did not frequent it. In any case Fatima and him would be inconspicuous amongst the tourists and there were plenty of dark corners in which to hide. He had to be content with her clipped, 'OK,' at an arrangement to meet early afternoon the following Saturday inside the cistern.

It was a dismal day, with a bitter wind blowing sleet showers as Can set off across the sea in his dinghy. The Bosphorus was as turbulent as his thoughts. His first date, if it could be called that, with his darling and instead of whispering words of love into her ears he was going to shock her with the news that he was harbouring her long lost twin sister. How she would react and how she would respond to his plan to swap them, and how he was going to explain why he was proposing it, he had not worked out.

He arrived at the cistern's entrance half-an-hour early, paid the entry fee and descended stone steps down into its dimly lit cavernous depths. Whenever he entered this magical subterranean place he experienced an altered sense of being: a serene state where his anxieties ceased to exist. He began to walk along one of the raised wooden platforms, mingling with the tourists, drips of water dropping onto his head from the vaulted ceiling. He watched ghostly carp patrolling the water underneath the platforms and marvelled, as he always did, at the multitude of finely carved columns, arranged with perfect symmetry, spreading throughout the chamber. He stood entranced, gazing as the columns lit up synchronistically, while classical music echoed from the brick-domed ceiling.

Realising it was nearly time for his meeting Can retraced his steps, still feeling calm. He did not see Fatima at first. She was standing in partial shadow near the bottom of the entrance steps, when suddenly the lights illuminated her face, making his heart lurch. He went towards her. 'Fatima! I'm so glad you've come,' he said, kissing her on both cheeks with no resistance, smelling her divine, musk-scented skin.

'Did you think I wouldn't come?' she replied, with no attempt at polite greetings.

Can was saddened by her antagonism and hoped that the cistern's special atmosphere would begin to affect her. 'I was simply hoping that you would come,' he said and then suggested that they stroll through the cistern.

'Yes, let's do that, Can. I love this place almost as much as Hudai's tomb – do you know it? It transports me into another, more peaceful place.' Can felt himself relax – *maybe this was going to be easier than he had thought.*

'I have heard of the saint Hudai's tomb but have never visited it. Maybe we can go together some time?'

Fatima thought of Gemma and her desire to go with her to the tomb. 'Maybe,' she responded with little enthusiasm. By this time they had reached the rear of the cistern where two columns were supported by stone Medusas, their heads emitting a greenish glow.

Can stopped and pointed at the heads, which were a little apart. 'It is a mystery why one of these heads is arranged sideways, while the other is upside-down.'

'Why they are here at all is very strange,' Fatima said, staring hard at the upside-down head. 'People say that the builders believed that if the head were placed upside down, it would ward off evil spirits.'

'Yes, but why is the other head sideways?'

'There are evil forces living in the snakes on Medusa's head and these would be empowered if both heads had the same position – at least, that's what folk say.'

'Oh, I see. I wish it were that easy in real life,' said Can, wiping a drop of water from his brow.

'What do you mean?'

'If we could only prevent evil forces from being unleashed by doing something simple, like placing heads in different positions.'

'Hmm, yes, I understand, and you know more than most people about evil forces, don't you?'

Can began to walk away from the Medusas, aware that there were several visitors nearby. 'Believe me, Fatima, I wish that I didn't. It's only because of my father . . .'

'Right, just blame it on your dad,' Fatima said, before Can could finish.

'Please Fatima, try to understand. I was born into the organisation, brought up by its Turkish leader. How can I extricate myself from it?'

Fatima looked directly into his eyes, making him melt inside. 'If you are strong enough, you can overpower anything, no matter how wicked.'

Can looked helplessly at her. 'Maybe you can help me to achieve this, Fatima.'

'With God's will, anything is possible,' she said as they walked towards a quieter, darker part of the cistern.

Can hoped that God would be on his side as he took a deep breath. 'I have something to tell you, Fatima. Something which might shock you,' he began.

'I am not easily shocked, Can,' Fatima said, looking closely at him in the flickering light.

'OK, well, I hope you won't think badly of me when I tell you what I've done.'

'You are making me curious. Please tell me now.'

'Right. I was sitting on the Karaköy ferry a week past Wednesday and a young woman approached me selling packets of tissues.'

'Wait! I have also met this girl. She looks identical to me, right?'

Can looked at Fatima's excited face with pleasure and continued. 'Right, yes. She could be your twin.'

'This is what I thought. I've always felt that I had a twin.'

'She spoke with a Kurdish accent, just like you and she told me that she came from the east, the same as you.'

'Yes, well your dear father told me that you know all about my past so I guess I don't need to tell you anything,' Fatima responded, a glint of anger in her eyes.

'Please don't be angry with me, Fatima. I can't help what the organisation knows,' said Can, before continuing. 'This girl, whose name is Fulya, was homeless so I took her for a meal in a *lokanta* in Karaköy.'

'Why did you do that?' Fatima was nervously twisting a lock of her hair now.

'Because I wanted to find out more about her and also I had an idea.'

'An idea? What sort of an idea?'

'I thought that she could be you when my father decides to begin the dancing activity, you know what I mean?'

'What? This is a preposterous plan! Have you told her about it?'

'Yes, I have and she seems to like the idea – in fact she'd like to become involved in the dealing.'

'Oh! So my so-called twin sister has criminal tendencies,' Fatima said, a shocked look on her face.

'Yes, I'm afraid that does seem to be so. Anyway, she is now living on my yacht and . . .'

'Your yacht!' Fatima's mouth gaped open, her eyebrows shooting up.

'Yes, well, it's not really mine and I only live on it from time to time. As I was saying, I've bought her some clothes and a belly dance outfit. She dances well, but not as well as you, and also she needs to put on some weight so I'm giving her lots of food.'

'It sounds like she's got it made – from being a homeless seller of tissues to living on a luxury yacht with nice clothes and plenty of food, not to mention a handsome host,' Fatima said sarcastically.

'Thanks for the "handsome host" bit, Fatima, but let me assure you that I am being an honourable one. I would not dream of touching Fulya. She might look like you, but she is not you.' Can's voice tailed off as he wondered whether or not to declare his love. *Not yet, it's too soon,* he told himself.

'So, what do you want me to do?' Fatima asked, ignoring the implication that Can found her attractive.

'I'd like you to teach her your dance moves, the ones that she doesn't know.'

'So, I'm going to have to meet her, aren't I?'

'I know you don't want to meet and neither does she, but it's the only way.'

'And where am I supposed to teach her my dance moves?'

Can longed for a smoke, but it was forbidden in the cistern, so he began fiddling with his car keys instead. 'The obvious place is on my yacht.'

'It might be obvious to you, Can, but not to me. This whole story may simply be a way to get me onto your yacht.'

'And why would I want to do that?' Can was becoming irritated with their discussion and Fatima's lack of trust in him.

'You tell me!' Fatima hissed.

Can attempted to steer the conversation onto safer ground. 'If you were to meet Fulya, then you would believe me, wouldn't you?'

'I guess so.'

'OK, we can meet in a café near the yacht. I've already discussed this with Fulya and I asked her to cover up completely, but she doesn't want to do it.'

'Why must she cover up?'

'Because I can't risk being seen with both of you.'

'You are so paranoid, Can.'

'I know. It's because I've been brought up to always be on guard. Anyway, would you be willing to wear the niqab and burka?'

'This would not be a problem for me. I have worn them at times in my past and I actually have them at home,' said Fatima, surprising Can considerably. He did not think that being a belly dancer and a devout Muslim went together.

'That's wonderful, Fatima. *Çok teşekkür ederim.* I think you should meet her soon because your special dancing could begin at any time. When are you free?'

'How about Monday morning? I know a secluded café in Ortaköy, near the mosque. It's a popular place but I think we can meet safely there and we can easily find it.'

'All right. Please give me the name and directions. Also may I have your home phone number?' Fatima scribbled the information on a piece of paper and Can slipped it into his wallet. They began to walk together towards the entrance until Can stopped and said, 'I think we should separate now, Fatima. It's been great to see you and I look forward to our next meeting.'

'I'm not sure that I'm looking forward to it, but I'll be there,' Fatima said before she hurried up the steps and disappeared into the crowds. Can stayed a little longer, conjuring up her face, her voice, her smell. *Only two days and I'll see her again, but only her eyes peering out from behind her niqab.*

FOURTEEN

Fatima got off the bus in Ortaköy early on Monday morning. It was not yet time to meet Can and Fulya so she made her way across the square outside the splendid Ortaköy Mosque, which sits right beside the Bosphorus, near the first bridge. Flocks of pigeons pecked at seed bought in paper packets from an old woman sitting outside the mosque. A few fishermen were selling their catch, displayed on bright red boards at the water's edge; gulls hovered above, hoping for some scraps and stray cats sat nearby watching, ready to pounce. It was a fine but chilly day and old men sat on benches, well wrapped up, smoking and staring out to sea or chatting with their neighbours. Fatima entered the mosque, covered in black as promised, and sat down on one of the large window ledges. Sunlight flooded in to the carpeted interior where a few men were praying towards Mecca at the front, their white skull caps bobbing up and down. Fatima sat, eyes closed, her hands resting, palms up, on her lap. Her breathing slowed as she went deep into meditation, her troubles temporarily suspended.

Rousing herself she rose and went outside, blinking in the sunlight, awakening to the cool sea breeze. The café was in a side street away from the square which was lined with trendier places and classy bars and restaurants. Can and Fulya were there already, sitting drinking coffee in an alcove at the rear. Fatima approached their table hesitantly, telling the waiter that she was meeting friends. Can turned and saw her, taking in her blackness and searching her dark eyes, which were fixed on Fulya. He jumped up. '*Hoş geldiniz, Fatima.* Please sit here beside your sister.' Fatima remained standing, staring at Fulya, who stared back, unable to speak. Can broke the silence by asking Fatima what she would like to drink. He took the opportunity to order another coffee at the counter, deciding that the twins needed some space.

As soon as he was gone Fatima sat down, reached out and touched Fulya's hand, feeling her answering grasp. 'Can you really be my twin?' Fatima said, her voice low, her eyes never leaving Fulya's.

'I can only see your eyes, but I feel you are my sister.'

'I did not want to meet you, but now that I have, there are so many questions, I do not know where to start.' Fulya began twisting a piece of her dark hair. *I do the exact same thing*, Fatima marvelled.

'I feel just the same,' Fulya laughed, adding, 'but then I would, wouldn't I?'

Can returned, relieved to find them both laughing, their voices mingling perfectly together.

'So, Fatima, do you believe me now?' he asked, a mischievous glint in his eyes.

'OK, I think you win, Can. For now at any rate.'

'I have been with Can for five days now, Fatima, and I think he is trustworthy.'

Fatima took a sip of coffee, careful not to get it on her veil, before saying, 'But what about you, Fulya? Can I trust you?'

'If you can't trust your twin, who can you trust?'

'Indeed, but I do not know you and I have faith in no-one, except God.'

'God? I do not know about Him – does He even exist?' said Fulya.

Before Fatima could respond, Can held up his hands. 'Enough!' he ordered. 'You can discuss God in detail on another occasion. For now we need to talk about the dancing.'

'OK, Can,' Fatima said, treating him to a reassuring smile. 'Do you really want to learn my dance moves so that you can take my place?' Fatima looked with interest at her twin, who was still fiddling with a lock of her hair.

'Yes, and now that I've met you, I want to even more. I can't wait to really see you and to look at us both, dressed in our costumes, in the mirror.'

'Right, is that agreed then?' Can asked.

'Yes,' the twins said in unison.

'Are you willing to do this on my yacht, Fatima?'

Fatima sat in silence for a few moments before replying, 'Yes, I will come to the yacht. In fact I could come today. I do not dance on Mondays and I also have tomorrow off.'

'Fantastic! Then you can accompany us back now? You'll have

your own cabin and there's everything you'd need for the night. I'll buy some more food and drink on the way and another dance costume,' Can said, hardly believing that he would have her company for two whole days.

*

When they reached the place where the yacht was moored, Fatima was impressed by its size, finally believing that Can had not been spinning her a tale. He held out his hand to steady her as she got into the dinghy, holding up the hem of her burka. Once the three of them plus the provisions were in the boat it was very full, but fortunately the sea was calm and Can easily rowed them out to the yacht. He climbed up the ladder first, then held out his hand again as Fatima neared the top, Fulya close behind her. Fulya gave Fatima a guided tour of the boat while Can unpacked the food and prepared lunch.
'What a luxurious *gulet*,' Fatima enthused.
'I know. I can still hardly believe that I am living here.'
'Yes, but for how long?'
'I don't know, but does it matter? I live each day as it comes.'
'This is certainly the way to live. Only Allah knows our destiny,' her twin responded.
'Oh, there you go talking about God again,' Fulya laughed.
'We shall talk about this more later, *inşallah*. We have much to discuss,' said Fatima. She went into her cabin to change and emerged dressed similarly to her sister, in black jogging trousers with a T-shirt and maroon fleece: the standard supplied guest apparel. When she appeared at the saloon dining table, which Can and Fulya were laying, they both stopped and stood, mouths agape.
Can shook his head, as if to dislodge the vision. 'I've drunk no alcohol, but I'm seeing double,' he gasped.
The twins looked carefully at each other in wonderment. 'We really are identical,' Fulya said.
'It's true, but you do need to put on some weight,' Fatima observed.
'Yes, girls, please sit and eat,' Can said, recovering his composure. The twins needed no encouragement and temporarily stopped talking to fill their stomachs. Afterwards they cleared up while Can sat smoking and thinking.

'Will we begin the lessons this afternoon?' Fulya asked as she washed the dishes.

'Yes, we must make the most of this time. The special belly dancing could begin soon,' Fatima said.

'So, you have no idea when it will start?'

'No. I guess Mehmet Bey, my boss, will tell me.'

'But surely Can will know?'

Can entered the galley, in search of a glass of water. 'Will know what?'

'When this belly dancing with drugs will happen,' Fulya said.

'Hopefully I will know, but Serkan Bey does not always tell me things.'

'But he's your father,' Fatima pointed out.

'Your father!' Fulya exclaimed, turning from the sink to stare at Can.

'Yes, sorry Fulya, I didn't tell you,' he muttered.

'Why ever not? Maybe there are other things you haven't told me?'

'Yes, why didn't you tell her?' Fatima joined in.

'I don't know. I suppose I didn't want to upset her.'

'Well, you've upset me now. Why doesn't your father tell you things?' Fulya persisted.

Can lit a cigarette and inhaled deeply before replying. 'Probably because he doesn't trust me.'

'Oh. So if your dad doesn't trust you, why should we?' said Fulya.

'Because, as I've told you, I am an honourable person. I didn't choose to be born into this organisation and my father knows that I do not agree with what they do.'

'I can understand that, can't you Fulya?' Fatima said.

'I suppose so,' her twin reluctantly agreed. 'Let's get these belly dance costumes on,' she said, smiling at her sister as she went into her cabin. Fatima followed her and their mood lifted as they tried on their clothes, giggling as if it were simply a game. Once they were finished they stood side by side, wearing the turquoise outfits, and gazed at themselves in the wardrobe's mirror.

Fatima was the first to break their silence. 'We're incredible,' she breathed, turning to look at Fulya, and then back again to their mirror images.

'Yes, it's quite uncanny, isn't it? I just need a bit more flesh on my stomach and thighs and we'll be identical. Let's go and see what Can thinks.'

Can was sitting reading the newspaper in the saloon. The twins approached quietly, then stood in the doorway and gave a tiny, unified cough. They were rewarded by his low whistle of appreciation as he examined each of them, looking for differences. 'Wow! You really are identical. You just need to fill out a bit more, Fulya.'

'Yes, and become as good a dancer as my sister.'

My sister! Only a short time ago I did not want to meet her, and now I feel a thrill when she calls me her sister, Fatima thought, then said out loud, 'We'd better start the teaching then, Can. Would you put on some suitable music?' Can willingly obliged and soon the yacht reverberated with the pulsating beat of belly dance music.

'May I stay and watch?' he asked.

The girls looked at each other, then nodded their heads. Fatima began, as she had with Gemma, by first observing what Fulya could do. She knew some different moves which came from Eastern Turkey and Fatima realised that it would not take long to teach her the ones she did not know, such as the backbend and other floor work. They danced until darkness fell and the lights from the Asian shore were glimmering on the Bosphorus. Tantalising aromas from the galley were arousing their appetites. 'It smells like our handsome host is making something tasty,' Fulya said, rolling her eyes.

'Hmm – he'd make a good husband for someone.'

'Do you fancy him yourself, sis?'

'Don't call me "sis",' Fatima exploded. 'No, I was thinking for you, Fulya.'

'I think it's you he likes.'

'Well, that's too bad because I don't fancy him. We're identical so he should like us both.'

'Yes, you would think so, but it doesn't seem to work like that.'

Can's head appeared above the galley's swing door. 'What are you gossiping about girls? It's dinner time.' He had heard snippets of their chatter, which had only increased his longing for Fatima. He carried in a steaming dish of shish kebab: grilled pieces of tender chicken on a skewer, and set it on the table, along with a bowl of salad and another of rice. He lit two tall candles and placed two bottles of red wine and crystal glasses in the table's centre.

'You have been busy, Can,' Fatima said.

'It is my pleasure to serve you,' he replied, trying to look into her eyes, but she did not respond. Fatima noticed that Fulya was attempting to make eye contact with him and was gratified when he eventually succumbed to her dark-eyed gaze. They were all hungry and Can made sure that Fulya got extra helpings. Fatima slowly sipped her wine watching as Can replenished his glass and then Fulya's. She was pleased with how the afternoon's teaching had gone and hoped that after another long session the next day that it would be enough. Once again the twins cleared the table and did the dishes. Fatima made *çay* which she offered to Can. 'I'm going out on deck to smoke and drink this. Would you like to bring yours?' he asked Fatima.

'It's a bit chilly out there. I'll stay inside with Fulya,' she said, noting the disappointment on his face. What could she do? She was longing to see Gemma again and was praying that she would come to the restaurant on Wednesday. After finishing their tea, the twins bid their host good night and retired to their cabins to enjoy the luxury of fluffy towels and soft linen sheets. Can sat smoking and drinking on deck wishing that he was elsewhere.

After breakfast the twins resumed their dancing and continued until lunch time. Can had once again prepared a feast which they ate outside, wrapped up against the cold. The sun was shining and they felt invigorated by the fresh air after their exertions. 'I'll have to head home later today,' Fatima said.

'I can give you a lift. What time would you like to leave?'

'Well, I think I still need to teach Fulya some more moves, so around four would do.'

'Can I come to? You'll be wearing your burka again, won't you Fatima?' said Fulya, looking expectantly at Can.

'Yes, that's fine, Fulya. You need to have a break from the yacht.'

'Thanks, Can. I'm suffering from a bit of cabin fever,' Fulya chuckled.

*

The twins sat in the back of the Mercedes as it purred along. It was the busiest time of day, the schools having just finished, and the streets were clogged with cars, their horns blaring, as impatient drivers tried to negotiate their way through the throng. 'I never had time to really talk with you,' Fatima told Fulya. 'There are so many questions in my head.'

'Me too,' agreed her sister, 'but maybe we shouldn't go there. It might stir up too many unpleasant memories.'

'You're right, Fulya, but nevertheless I still want to see you again.'

Can observed them in the mirror and said, 'I'm going to come and watch you dance tomorrow evening, Fatima.'

'Oh, will your other pals be there?' Fatima asked, frowning.

'I'm not sure, but I think I should go,' Can said.

'May I come too?' Fulya butted in.

'No! You can't be seen anywhere near your sister,' Can said in exasperation.

'But what if I wore the burka?'

Fatima laughed. 'That's a crazy idea, Fulya. Burka-clad females don't usually go to watch belly dance shows.'

'Well, maybe just this one time?' her sister pleaded.

Fatima squeezed her twin's arm affectionately. 'I don't see how this could be done. Can couldn't be seen with you – it would arouse the Mafia's suspicions if they were there and you couldn't sit alone. That's not the done thing for any Turkish women, especially devout ones.'

'I understand, but I really want to come.'

Suddenly Fatima had an idea. 'If Gemma is coming then I suppose you could masquerade as one of her students. She could sit with you when she's not dancing.'

'Then you'd have to tell Gemma who the burka-clad woman is, Fatima. That's not a good idea – no-one must know about Fulya and our plan except us.' Can could only see Fatima's eyes peering out of her niqab in the mirror, but he saw a shiftiness within them.

Fatima took a deep breath: she did not want Can to know anything about Gemma and she cursed herself for her sudden idea. She would just tell him as little as possible. 'Gemma met Fulya selling tissues and noticed our similarity. She told me and I said that I had met her too, but that's all. I can phone her when I get home and explain that we've now met and she'd like to come to the restaurant.'

'But what about the burka? How can you explain that? She was dressed very differently when she was selling tissues,' Can said.

'Don't worry, Can. I won't tell Gemma anything, but she's my friend and can be discreet.'

'Come on, Can. Just this once, please,' Fulya begged.

The combined pressure of the twins forced Can to capitulate. 'OK, Fulya, only once, but you must give no indication that you know me or Fatima. You must keep your speech to the minimum. I'll drop you some distance from the restaurant and give you directions. Only if you agree to my terms will I let you do this.'

'OK, thanks Can,' Fulya said excitedly.

By this time they were nearing Fatima's apartment. 'Come up with me and I'll give you the burka and phone Gemma,' she said.

Can parked the Mercedes round the corner from Fatima's flat and waited for Fulya's return. 'Don't be long,' he told her retreating back.

Gemma answered immediately when her phone rang. 'Oh, Fatima, it's so good to hear your voice.'

'Are you coming tomorrow evening?' Fatima asked.

'Yes, I am and I'll be bringing an ex-student, Hasan,' Gemma said, too brightly.

Hasan? Who is this man? Will it still be safe for Fulya to go? These thoughts buzzed busily in Fatima's brain as she tried to absorb the information. 'That's funny, because someone else is coming and I'd like you to pretend that she's one of your students.'

'This sounds most mysterious, Fatima.'

'Yes, I know. You remember the tissue seller on the ferry? Well, we've now met and she wants to see me dance. She'll be wearing a burka, so that we're not seen together. I can't say any more right now, but please don't tell anyone who she really is.'

'OK Fatima. I won't say anything to anyone, including Hasan,' Gemma reassured her.

'Great. I've got to go now and I look forward to dancing with you tomorrow,' Fatima said and hung up.

'Is everything all right?' Fulya asked.

'Yes, she's going but an ex-student of hers, Hasan, will also be coming, which makes things difficult.'

'Oh, right. Well, I'm just going to have to practise my acting.'

'Yes, but please be careful. Also don't mention Hasan to Can – he'd probably stop you going.'

'OK, sis. I'll see you tomorrow,' Fulya said, kissing Fatima goodbye.

On her return to the car she told Can that everything was arranged for the following evening and he said little as he drove them back to the yacht, sad that his darling was not accompanying them.

FIFTEEN

The weather suited Fatima's mood the next morning. A steady drizzle seeped from a leaden sky, the air bitterly cold. She got up late and sat brooding about Gemma as she drank her coffee. She had been longing to hold her close again, but would this ever happen? Then there was Fulya. She still couldn't quite believe that she had met her twin and the whole time on Can's yacht seemed like a dream. Even though they had never met, except in their mother's womb, there was a deep understanding between them, which was almost telepathic. Despite this she could not understand Fulya's keenness to become involved in the drug trafficking – it could not simply be that she wanted to protect her sister, no, she had her own agenda, and Fatima did not entirely trust her.

The bus journey to Taksim Square in the late afternoon was dreadful. There were no seats and she stood, sandwiched between people wearing thick coats, scarves and hats, all of which steamed gently in the warm interior, the air filled with a pungent smell of damp wool and stale sweat, a faint whiff of cologne occasionally improving the atmosphere when someone got off. When she finally joined the crowds outside in the square, she felt like having another shower. It was raining harder and she raised her umbrella, battling through the throngs to the restaurant.

She pushed open the door and entered the warm interior, glad to be dry. Before she had even closed her umbrella, Mehmet Bey came to greet her. The restaurant was empty, waiting for the evening rush and Fatima's boss followed her into her changing room. One look at his face immediately filled her with dread. 'Fatima, I've been told to expect our special guests tonight,' he began, his eyes ringed by dark shadows, their haunted look arousing her pity.

'You mean the Mafia, don't you?'

'Yes, if you must call them that, but I think it would be safer to refer to them as our special guests.'

'OK, if that's what you want,' Fatima replied, removing her wet coat.

'Yes, it is. Tonight I have reason to believe that they will try out this business of trafficking drugs, via your dance costume. You will give them to me in the breaks and I will pass them on to others later.' Mehmet combed his fingers through his hair, watching Fatima nervously.

'Exactly how will they do this without causing suspicion?'

'I think small amounts of compacted heroin will be used, say one or two grams. These will be wrapped in a lira note and sealed in a plastic sachet. This way they will be easily concealed in your bodice or waistband.'

'I'll have to be careful not to drop them,' Fatima said, her expression tense.

'Absolutely! It will only be the five men who you saw before that are going to do it tonight. It's an experiment and if it goes well there might be more dealers the next time.'

'I don't want this, Mehmet, but like you, they have a hold on me so I'll have to comply, but what do I get out of it?'

'I told you before that you would make more money than you usually receive in tips, a lot more if this is a success.'

'What about the private show that they wanted?'

'I'm not sure. They might want it later.'

'Do you know that Gemma is coming tonight?'

'No, I didn't, but I thought that it was possible. Serkan Bey knows that she sometimes dances here Wednesday evenings, in fact that's why he chose tonight.'

'Why has he done that? Surely with Gemma here it's more dangerous – she might notice something.'

'He thinks that she'll be a distraction. They won't use her for the drugs and the customers will be watching her while they're stuffing packets down your bodice,' Mehmet said with a shrug.

'This whole business is ridiculous! They are putting themselves into a position where they could be arrested.'

'I know what you mean, Fatima, but they have so much power, they feel invulnerable.'

'Well, I hope that they are proved wrong.'

'But if they are, Fatima, we are also in trouble.'

'Remember what I told you before, Mehmet Bey? We must be strong and trust in God to help us. We are both good people and we will triumph.' She sat down on her stool and began to make up her face.

'I hope you are right. I'll leave you to prepare and please take special care again with your face, your costume and your dancing. *Iyi şanslı,* good luck,' he said, softly closing her door.

*

Fatima had just finished making up her face when there was another knock on her door. 'Come in,' she cried and turned to see Gemma's sweet face peering around it.

'*Merhaba*, Fatima. Would you like to meet Hasan?'

'Of course, Gemma.'

Gemma opened the door wide to reveal a tall young man dressed in black jeans and a polo-necked grey jumper. 'This is Hasan,' she announced.

Hmm. He's rather attractive with his curly brown hair and kind eyes. But the way he's looking at her – ugh! 'Pleased to meet you, Hasan,' she said, as politely as she could, holding out her hand.

He shook it firmly. 'I'm pleased to meet you too, Fatima. I've heard so much about you.' *I bet you haven't heard that much about me,* Fatima thought, giving Gemma a penetrating look.

'Right, Hasan, you'll need to leave us to get dressed,' Gemma said.

'OK, I'll go and get a drink.'

As soon as he'd gone Gemma tried to start telling Fatima about him, but she was interrupted.

'There's no time to discuss Hasan now, Gemma. First, could you go and see if Fulya, that's the tissue seller, is here? She'll be wearing a burka, remember?'

'What if there's more than one burka-clad woman?'

'Don't be silly, Gemma. This isn't the time for jokes. If she's there you'll need to introduce her to Hasan as another of your ex-students.'

'What if he asks any awkward questions?'

'Just leave it to my twin. She says she's an excellent actress.' Gemma disappeared into the restaurant where she spotted a lone female sitting at the back clad in black. She quickly introduced herself and then Hasan, leaving the two of them together. Back in the changing room she hurriedly began to do her face. 'Let me do that,' Fatima said and Gemma meekly complied, relishing her friend's closeness, the touch of her fingers, her entrancing smell. Fatima worked in silence for a few minutes also delighting in Gemma's nearness. But her anger was bubbling just below the surface and suddenly she could no longer contain it. 'Why did you come with this Hasan? Is he your boyfriend?'

Gemma turned to look at her friend. 'Please don't be angry with me. I will try to explain. Let's meet tomorrow and you can also tell me all about your twin – it's so exciting.'

'OK, that's if we survive this night,' Fatima whispered.

'Whatever do you mean?' Fatima quickly told Gemma about the drugs, warning her not to tell anyone, including Hasan. Gemma promised to keep everything secret as she dressed once more in the scarlet costume, Fatima resplendent in a tangerine-coloured one. Soon the signal for them to enter came and they went onto the dance floor together, to rapturous applause. Many of the customers had been at Gemma's first performance and they were pleased to see her again.

Right in front, as before, sat the five Mafia men, clad in the same black suits, grey shirts and black ties. Can sat next to his father, who was accompanied by Natalia, wearing a silvery, figure-hugging dress with diamonds adorning her throat, wrists and ring fingers, her blonde hair loose around her shoulders. Fatima swept the group with her dark eyes, briefly settling on Can's with a fathomless glance, before she glided towards Serkan Bey and wobbled her breasts close to his face. In response she felt his smooth fingers slide a sachet deep into her cleavage. She repeated this ploy with each of the three other men, who also slid sachets down her breasts, over her erect nipples. When she came to Can she took extra care to arouse him, pouting her lips into a kiss, bending over him until her bosom touched his face. He buried himself in her flesh, smelling her warm, entrancing scent, at the same time stuffing another sachet between her breasts.

Meanwhile Gemma was playing the other tables, the customers placing notes in her costume with obvious pleasure. She made her way to where Hasan and Fulya were sitting silently watching the proceedings, a dish of melon and a bowl of mixed nuts in front of them. 'Hello Fulya, it was nice of you to come,' Gemma said slowly in English.

'Thank you my teacher,' Fulya managed, her dark eyes fixed on Gemma's.

'How are you two getting on?' Gemma asked Hasan in English.

'Not very well. She speaks little English and no Turkish, only Kurdish, which I can't understand.'

'That's too bad – you'll just have to watch me dancing.'

'Yes, I'm really enjoying that. You dance well and your friend, Fatima, she's putting on quite a show for those guys in the front.'

Before he could say any more Gemma danced away, noting that Fatima was still focussing on Can. She moved towards them and hissed in Fatima's ear, 'Time for a break.' They both bowed to the audience and went to their room. Once inside Fatima began to take the sachets out of her bodice. They made a neat pile on the dresser. 'Wow! That's quite a stash,' Gemma gasped.

Fatima quickly hid the packets in a draw and locked it. 'Remember to say nothing about this to anyone,' she warned Gemma.

'I won't but I'm a bit worried about Hasan. He commented about the length of time you spent with Can and company. That's why I came and broke it up.'

'OK, thanks for that, Gemma. When we go back I'll spread myself about more and you can dance for the guys.'

They re-entered the dance floor, once more to loud clapping and some whistles. Gemma began to perform some of her best moves in front of the Mafia, her hips rotating and her belly muscles rippling in time with the music. Their faces were expression-less, except for Can who pressed a note into her top with a wink. She danced away, allowing Fatima to take her place. The men's faces lit up and more sachets were pressed into her bra and waistband. As Serkan Bey slid one into her bodice he muttered, 'Make sure you give all these to Mehmet Bey. We have them counted.' Fatima nodded, a sliver of fear passing through her.

*

At the end of the evening Hasan came over to Gemma. 'Shall we give Fulya a lift home?' he asked.

Gemma thought quickly. 'No, her father's coming to collect her. I'll just get changed and then we can go.' Back in the changing room she arranged to meet Fatima for lunch the next day at the entrance to the Spice Bazaar, then left, clasping her hand and whispering, 'be careful.'

Mehmet Bey knocked on the door as soon as Gemma and Hasan had gone. 'How was that for you, Fatima?'

'Not as bad as I'd thought it might be,' she admitted.

'Good. Now I've got to count the sachets,' he said as Fatima unlocked the draw. 'All present and correct. Please take this.' He thrust a wad of notes into her palm.

'Thanks, Mehmet. This looks like a lot of money.' She squashed the cash into her bag.

'Keep this up and you'll get loads more,' he said, adding, 'I'll call you a taxi now.'

As Fatima hurried towards Taksim Square and her waiting cab she noticed a woman in a burka who she guessed was Fulya; she was partly hidden in a shop's darkened entrance. 'Is that you, Fulya?' she said in a low voice.

'Yes. I'm waiting for Can.'

'I'd wait with you but I have to get my taxi,' Fatima said, a look of concern on her face.

'It's OK. He'll be here soon. I'll phone you,' Fulya said, edging further into shadow.

As Fatima neared the end of the pedestrianised avenue she looked back and saw Can disappearing into the shop's doorway. *Please God, keep my sister safe,* she prayed.

SIXTEEN

There had been a light sprinkling of snow in the night and Gemma sat on the Eminönü ferry entranced by the distant mosques' silvery domes which were glinting in wintry sunshine. There were less people out and about and she made her way easily through the slush to a large underpass, where vendors were selling cheap clothes and household goods. She clambered up the steps to the Spice Bazaar, its ancient domes also powdered with snow. Fatima was waiting, huddled up in a thick woollen coat and fur boots, her hair hidden under a red woolly hat, a long black scarf around her neck. Gemma was similarly swaddled and they exclaimed about the snow as they greeted each other with kisses on their frozen cheeks.

'Are you hungry yet?' Fatima asked.

'No, it's still early. Can we walk a little first? I love this place,' Gemma said as they entered the bazaar's airy interior with its high domed roof, a mellow yellow glow from the ceiling adding to a profusion of colours, smells and sights.

'I love it too.' Fatima paused to look at a brightly lit stall selling many different kinds of *lokum,* or Turkish Delight. 'My favourite is this pistachio-filled one,' she told Gemma, who accepted a sample from the vendor, his brown eyes smiling and bushy moustache twitching in anticipation of a sale. Gemma bought a half kilo box and pressed it into her friend's gloved hands, despite her protestations.

'We can eat it together later,' she promised.

Next they were assailed by the sweet aroma of dried fruits: mounds of figs, apricots, dates, prunes, sultanas and raisins, alongside which were nuts: hazel, brazil, pistachio, peanut, cashew and others. When Gemma admitted that hazelnuts were her favourite Fatima gave her a brown paper bag of them, with a look deep into her eyes which made Gemma's heart begin to pound.

There were so many different spices and herbs, all beautifully arranged in neat piles, some herbs hanging from hooks high above.

Sellers deftly measured out scoops of the powders into bags on manual scales, passing them to customers with charming smiles. 'I don't know what half of these are,' Gemma admitted, peering at the Turkish labels.

'I can identify some of the herbs from when I lived in the east, but I only know their Turkish names.'

'Oh, I'm going to have to buy some of this,' Gemma exclaimed as they came to a place selling slabs of honeycomb, the dark golden syrup oozing from them. A tall, broad-shouldered man carefully cut a slice, wrapped it in greaseproof paper, placed it in a polythene bag and gave it to Gemma, with an *afiyet olsun.*

At the far end of the bazaar's main street the air was filled with the heady aroma of fresh coffee beans. Numerous varieties were on display, varying in size and darkness. Fatima chose some dark brown beans which the vendor whizzed in a grinder, adding to the incredible smell. 'All these smells and sights are making me hungry,' Gemma said.

'Me too. There's a small *büfe* along that road,' Fatima replied, heading away from the coffee stall along another street where tourist souvenirs were prominently displayed. A tempting whiff of doner kebab increased their appetites as they entered the *büfe* and sat at a white plastic table with matching chairs by the front window. 'I'm going to have Iskender Kebab. They do a really tasty one here,' Fatima said.

'Right, I'll have one too and a glass of *ayran.*'

They watched the chef slicing thin slivers of lamb off of a vertical, rotating grill, then spreading them on a layer of diced *pide* bread. He poured savoury tomato sauce and browned butter over it, placed a dollop of yoghurt on the side and a sprinkling of parsley on top. The waiter placed the steaming plates in front of the girls along with two glasses of *ayran.* 'Hmm, this looks so good and smells delicious,' Gemma said, taking her first mouthful. They ate in silence, savouring the food while watching the busy scene outside. A group of Russian tourists dressed in expensive furs were haggling over pieces of silver jewellery in the shop opposite, while a head-scarfed Turk rummaged through a pile of towels outside another establishment.

Once they had finished eating they ordered Turkish coffee and while waiting for it to brew, Gemma tried to broach the subject of

Hasan. 'Fatima, please don't be upset about Hasan,' she began.

Her friend quickly interrupted. 'I am not upset as long as you are happy, dear Gemma.'

'I am happiest when I'm with you, Fatima.' Gemma grasped her friend's now warm and gloveless hand. 'I began to see Hasan after our night together. I was, and still am, confused. I am attracted to men but I find you irresistible – I've never felt like this about anybody before.'

'I feel exactly the same. I can't wait to hold you in my arms again. Could you come home with me today?'

'I'd love to but I've got lessons first thing tomorrow morning, I'm afraid.' Gemma turned to the waiter who had arrived with their coffee and said, 'thank you.'

'I'm not working tonight. Mehmet Bey has given me the night off after last night. Could I stay with you?'

Gemma frowned. 'I'm not sure. Tina might not like it.'

'Are you worried that she'll think you'll try and make out with her next?' Fatima chuckled, turning her coffee cup upside down on its saucer. 'You do the same, Gemma, and I'll tell our fortunes.'

Gemma carefully turned over her cup. 'She knows I fancy men and I've never showed that sort of interest in her, so I guess not.'

'That's OK then. She doesn't need to know anything any way.'

'Of course you're right, *canım*,' Gemma smiled. 'You can come back with me then.'

'Wonderful!' Fatima's eyes shone as she squeezed Gemma's hand. 'Right, let me tell our fortunes.' She turned her cup back and stared hard at the patterns left by the coffee. 'Hmm. I can see great pleasure for tonight but later, you see here, there is some turbulence. It is unclear but I am sure there will be a happy ending.'

'Right, now do mine,' Gemma said turning her cup upright again. Fatima took her time peering intently at the coffee swirls and Gemma began to feel annoyed. 'What is it? What do you see?' she cried, trying to look into the cup.

'Patience, my dear. I must concentrate. This picture is full of contradictions and uncertainties. On the one hand it says that you will have a long, happy and prosperous life, but conversely I see sadness, poverty and death.'

'Great! Thanks, Fatima.'

'*Merak etme.* Don't worry. It will all work out.'

'I hope you're right. Now, please tell me all about your twin.'

Fatima described everything that had happened, from Can finding Fulya, to the yacht and finally to the previous night. 'Wow! That's quite a story,' Gemma said when she had finished.

'Yes, it is and I'm still trying to process it. I'm also worried about her.'

'You mean if she dances like you did last night?'

'Yes. She seems reckless, wanting to drug deal herself. Unlike me, she's got nothing to lose. Even if they discover something bad in her past, it won't matter to her. She has no job, no home, no family here. She ran away from Diyarbakır when something dreadful happened to her, I'm sure.'

'When will you see her again?'

'I don't know. She said she'd phone me, but there's no phone on the yacht and if she does the dancing then I can't be there.'

'Unless you wear the burka,' Gemma smirked.

'They would become too suspicious seeing a burka-clad woman there again.'

'I suppose so, but I could be dancing too and I'd tell you what happens.'

'That's true and they want you to be there – as long as you're safe, dear Gemma.'

'I'll be OK, despite your gloomy fortune telling. Shall we go to Kadıköy now?' Gemma said, beckoning to the waiter to pay the bill.

'Let me pay that,' Fatima insisted. 'I got paid lots of money last night.'

'I hope you've changed it into dollars already.'

'Yes, I did that this morning and put it into my savings account.'

'That's good. The rate of inflation is astronomical. I get fed up with battling to change my salary at the end of every month. Often the exchange offices run out of hard currency there are so many people queueing up for it then.'

'Just another problem about living in Turkey,' Fatima laughed as they went outside.

'There are many problems, it's true, but I love living here.'

'*İyi,* good. I love you living here too, Gemma.'

*

The weather had improved, the slushy streets dry again, with a subsequent increase in the crowds as they came out of the bazaar. The underpass was full of folk and Gemma linked her arm through Fatima's as they struggled through the masses, then up the steps to the ferry landings. Kadıköy was equally busy and they were relieved to finally reach Gemma's flat. There was no sign of Tina which pleased Gemma. She wanted Fatima to herself and Tina would have asked too many questions, some of which might have been tricky to answer.

'Would you like a glass of wine?' she offered as soon as they'd removed their coats and shoes. Gemma had quickly got used to the Turkish custom of slipping into slippers at the door and keeping a small supply for visitors. The streets were so dirty, especially in wet weather, it was the sensible thing to do.

'Yes please.' Fatima sat on the settee and stretched out her long legs with a contented sigh.

Gemma placed two glasses of *Villa Doluca* on the coffee table and sat next to her friend. They clinked glasses, '*Şerefe,*' they said in unison.

The phone rang and Gemma answered it. 'Hi, Hasan.' She made a face at Fatima as she listened to his voice. 'No, I'm busy right now. I'll speak to you later,' she said, ringing off.

'That was quite abrupt,' Fatima remarked.

'It was, wasn't it? I didn't know what to say,' Gemma said, feeling guilty.

'You didn't want to admit that I was here.'

'That's true but I don't know why.' Gemma took a large mouthful of wine.

'Because you're being unfaithful to him.' Fatima put her arm on Gemma's shoulders and bent to kiss her lips.

A jolt of desire passed through her. *Was she being unfaithful?* She supposed she was, but she hadn't thought of it like that. 'We'd better go to bed. Tina might come in,' she said, finishing her wine.

'OK, in a minute once I've drunk mine,' Fatima said, trying not to laugh at Gemma's awkwardness. Once the bottle was finished they quickly got ready for bed. Gemma left Tina a note that Fatima was there, hoping that she'd go to school before they arose in the morning.

The same wonderful feeling overwhelmed her as soon as she was in Fatima's embrace. It was unlike anything she had experienced with Hasan or her former boyfriends, it was like an awakening of some hidden longing. She surrendered to it and let the tide of passion engulf them once again. Gemma slept so deeply she did not hear Tina come in. She was still there at breakfast but they were so busy getting ready for work, there was little time to chat. They all left the apartment together and Gemma promised to phone Fatima about the following Wednesday evening.

To their surprise Mehmet Bey said nothing about any drug business and there was no sign of the Mafia men, including Can, that night. Hasan drove Gemma there again, so she had to return with him, making do with snatched embraces with Fatima in their changing room. 'I wonder if last week were a one-night phenomenon,' Gemma remarked at the end of the evening as they were removing their costumes.

'I pray that you are right,' Fatima said, clasping her hands together and whispering a prayer.

SEVENTEEN

Fulya was becoming bored with being on the yacht and stuffing her face. But, on the other hand, she had no wish to return to her homeless existence. *I should be thankful for this life of luxury,* she thought as she sat at the deck table after lunch, munching an apple and looking vaguely at the Asian shore. In the distance she spotted a tiny speck of a boat which gradually became larger until she could make out the figure of a man, his hands on the tiller, steering it in her direction. The small fishing boat drew alongside and its captain shouted, 'Is Can there?'

Fulya stood at the rail peering down at the man who she did not recognise. 'No, he isn't,' she said, wishing that he was.

'I know you,' the man continued, tying his boat to the bottom rung of the ladder. 'You're Fatima, the belly dancer.'

Fulya thought quickly. This man must have been sitting with Can at the front when her twin was dancing and receiving drugs. She had only seen his back. 'Oh, yes, I remember you now.'

'That was some show you put on for us. Is there a chance of a private performance now?'

Fulya's mind was racing, her heart hammering with fear. *Be careful! This man is dangerous – if you refuse he might beat you up, or worse.* 'It is possible. Come on up,' she said, in what she hoped was a soft, enticing voice.

The man clambered up the ladder. 'I'm Zeki Bey,' he said, holding out his hand and shaking hers in an iron-like grip. He was tall and broad-shouldered, strong and muscular, with mean-looking black eyes, short, black hair and a black pencil moustache. The black suit was gone, blue jeans and a thick jumper in its place.

Fulya did not like the look of him one bit. 'Pleased to meet you properly, Zeki Bey. You must be intelligent with a name like that.'

'Indeed, that is so,' he chuckled, his eyes on her breasts, just visible beneath her fleece.

'May I offer you something to drink?' Fulya asked, ignoring his lecherous stare.

'Whisky would be good if you have it,' he said, sitting down at the table. Fulya disappeared into the kitchen and returned with a full glass of the alcohol and a bowl of ice. For herself she brought a glass of water.

'You're not going to join me?' he asked, adding some ice to his glass.

'No, it's too early in the day for me.' Fulya looked directly into his eyes, trying to work him out.

'So, how come you are on this yacht? Are you Can's woman now?'

If I tell him I'm Can's woman, maybe he'll leave me alone, Fulya reasoned. 'Yes, I am,' she said emphatically.

'Well, Can's a sly one. He never told us.' Zeki took a swig of whisky and asked for another. Fulya brought the bottle and placed it on the table.

'Whoa! Are you trying to get me drunk, *canım*,' he said, lighting a cigarette.

Fulya laughed uncertainly. His use of '*canım*' had made her alert. 'No, of course not. Please enjoy,' she urged him.

Zeki topped up his glass and blew a smoke ring carefully towards her. 'I think Can will not mind if you give me a show. He's a generous fellow.'

Fulya gave him a long look. 'Can should be back any minute,' she said.

'That's OK. He won't mind,' Zeki assured her.

Fulya realised she was stuck. 'Shall I change into my costume?'

'Yes, please do. I want to see your curves. I may even stuff something into them,' he said, leering at her.

'OK, I'll go now and change,' Fulya said, opening the door.

'Don't be long,' Zeki ordered her retreating back.

In her bedroom she locked the door and began to get undressed, trying to calm her feeling of dread. She hoped that Can would not be long: he was often away on business and could return at any time. She quickly put on some make-up, trying to stop her hand from shaking as she applied black mascara to her already long, curly lashes and rouge to her already pink cheeks. She slipped into the turquoise outfit which she now filled out nicely, her curves as curvaceous as her sister's.

Zeki was standing at the railing, looking out to sea when she came onto the deck. He turned and let out a long, low whistle. 'Fantastic,' he gasped, gawping at her breasts, her belly, her buttocks as she wheeled around.

'Shall we go inside and I'll play some music?' Fulya fluttered her eyelids at him provocatively.

'OK. Your nipples are wonderfully erect, so I guess you are cold.'

Disregarding his comment Fulya led the way into the saloon where Zeki lounged on the settee, his whisky bottle and glass beside him. Despite her fear, Fulya was happy to dance and immediately the music began she was into the rhythm, her hips rotating, her belly rippling and her bosom bouncing. The man watched her every move, obviously aroused, his tongue almost hanging out. 'Come closer, *canım,*' he commanded and Fulya obeyed, swaying towards him. He reached out and touched her right breast, which she playfully withdrew.

'Naughty, naughty! To touch you must give me something,' she cooed.

'I'll give you something all right,' he muttered, grasped her breast and pushed a sachet of heroin deep within her bra.

'*Teşekkür ederim,* kind sir.' She thrust her left breast into his face, and, spluttering, he grabbed it and produced another sachet, almost ripping her bodice.

'Careful, or you'll have to buy me another outfit,' Fulya warned.

'Why, you cheeky bitch! I've given you enough dope to purchase several costumes, and more.' Fulya observed Zeki's face – it was an unpleasant shade of purple, perspiration shining on his forehead. The whisky bottle was almost empty and she wondered if he might pass out. She was cruelly awakened from her fantasy by a blow to her legs which made them buckle. She fell to the floor at his feet and he launched himself on top of her, tearing at her bodice and sucking her nipples til they were raw. He bit her breasts, then reached further down and began to pull at her long skirt. She struggled to be free but he was a dead weight upon her. 'Don't try to fight, you cow. I know you want it,' he gasped, fiddling with his belt, then zip.

He was about to unzip himself when a voice rang out. 'Stop right there!' Zeki ceased fumbling, his breathing coming in ragged gasps. He looked up and saw Can standing in the doorway, a pistol pointing at his head.

'Don't shoot, Can. Please!'

'Don't grovel, Zeki Bey, it doesn't suit you,' Can began, then stopped. Zeki's head had slumped between Fulya's breasts.

'Oh, my God! You've killed him,' Fulya screeched, trying to extricate herself without success.

'I haven't done anything. If I'd shot him, you would have heard it.'

'Get him off me Can – it's too horrible.'

Can bent down and with difficulty manoeuvred Zeki's bulk off of Fulya. His eyes were closed. Can felt his pulse, then checked for breathing. 'My God, you're right! He's dead. He must have had a heart attack.' He put away his gun, his face ashen.

'He'd drunk a lot of whisky and his face was purple,' Fulya said, scrambling to her feet, then sitting down fast on the sofa as her head swam. Can joined her, his head in his hands.

'What are we going to do?' he cried.

Fulya suddenly felt calm and in control. 'You'll take the yacht out to sea and then we can dump his body. Did he have any family? Anyone to miss him?'

'No, he wasn't married, although I'm sure his bastards are scattered all over the country. His only family were the Mafia and they'll miss him, but they won't search too closely.'

'That's settled then. It's getting dark now so we can go, but before we dump him we should remove his documents.' She found Zeki's wallet, stuffed with cash and credit cards, his passport and another bag containing more of the heroin sachets. 'Wow! We've got quite a haul here,' she said gleefully, adding, 'he wasn't so intelligent after all.'

With Fulya taking command of the situation, Can recovered himself. 'We'd better search his boat as well, then hide it on the beach.'

'OK, let's do that now,' said Fulya. In the boat they discovered another stash of heroin, hidden inside the small cabin, along with some papers. 'What was he doing with all this stuff?'

'Looks like he was doing a bit of trafficking on the side,' Can said.

'We'd better hide all this,' Fulya said, her eyes shining.

'I've got a secret place under the floor boards,' Can admitted. He carried the package onto the yacht and disappeared into the kitchen.

Fulya followed and was just in time to see where it was hidden. Can looked up at her as he knelt on the floor. 'Don't you go getting any funny ideas about taking any of this.'

'Don't worry, Can. I'm sure we can share it.'

Can decided to drop the subject – there were more important matters to be dealt with. 'Can you take the dinghy while I drive the boat to the shore?'

'Yes, no problem,' Fulya said. With that they clambered down the ladder again and set off for the land. Can moored the boat underneath some low hanging branches, then stepped ashore, water filling his rubber boots and wetting his trousers as he pulled them aside. He quickly joined Fulya in the dinghy and grabbed the oars, barely having time to register her ability to row. He was glad of the exertion. It prevented him from thinking about what they were going to do next.

Back on the yacht he started the engine and soon they were heading out into the middle of the Bosphorus. The sea was choppy and clouds scudded across a sliver of moon as he carefully navigated the vessel through the strait, avoiding large cargo ships, their lights twinkling, as well as smaller boats. He headed towards the Black Sea and when the channel began to widen he switched off the engine and let down the anchor. Without speaking he beckoned to Fulya and they began the ghastly and arduous task of dragging Zeki's lifeless body onto the deck. Once outside they straightened up, pausing to catch their breaths. At the rear of the yacht there was a ladder, which could be extended into the sea for swimming. Can put this in place and they both positioned the corpse so that it could slide down into the water. Just before committing Zeki to his watery grave they both mumbled a short prayer, then watched silently as he was swallowed up by the sea.

'*Bitti*,' Can said. It's finished. Fulya hoped it was. Can turned the yacht around and set a course back to their mooring place. Fulya stood at the rail, the wind tugging at her hair, glad to be free again. Once the yacht was safely settled Can joined her on deck, a cigarette dangling from his lips. 'How do you feel now?' he asked her.

'A bit bruised, but I'll live,' Fulya laughed.

'I don't know how you can laugh about it – it must have been awful.'

'Life is awful. You have to laugh at it to survive.'

'That's a sad viewpoint from one so young.'

'This is going to turn into a philosophical discussion if we're not careful, Can. I'm going to shower and change and you should do the same; you'll catch a chill in those damp clothes.' Can had forgotten he was wet. It must be the shock, he guessed.

Showered and in clean clothes they met in the saloon. 'Would you like a drink?' Can offered.

'A large whisky, please – that's if you have another bottle.'

'Yes, there should be one in the cabinet.' Can produced a bottle and poured some into the decanter. He gave Fulya a double and one for himself.

She took a big mouthful, swallowed and coughed. 'Oh! I'm not used to this stuff but I feel I need it,' she gasped, her eyes watering.

'We've both had a big shock. I'll bring us some nibbles to soak this up.' Fulya felt herself relax as the alcohol warmed her body; she took another sip, her head light. *Can is such a sweetie taking care of me,* she thought woozily. Can appeared carrying a tray with biscuits and cheese, nuts and dried fruit temptingly arranged on it and sat down next to Fulya. She roused herself to eat, surprised to discover that she was hungry. Can also tucked in, suddenly ravenous. They cleared the tray between them and then Can said, 'Fulya, no-one must know about tonight. Please tell nobody, especially your sister.'

'Naturally I will keep it a secret,' Fulya replied, simultaneously thinking that Fatima would sense that something was wrong.

'My father will comment on Zeki's disappearance but he probably knows that he was stealing heroin from us and dealing it himself. This would probably have resulted in his death sooner or later.'

'Well, that's all right then, isn't it?'

'I guess so, Fulya. You are quite a woman.'

Fulya leaned over and tenderly kissed Can on the cheek. '*Çok teşekkür ederim,*' she whispered. Can felt engulfed by her musky smell and almost thought she was Fatima, almost kissing her back. But he did not and simply smiled at her.

'I'm exhausted. Is it OK if I go to bed now, Fulya?'

'Yes, of course. We both need a good sleep.'

'Let's hope we get it,' Can said with an, '*iyi geceler.*'

EIGHTEEN

A week had passed since Zeki's death. Fulya had stayed on the yacht, trying to keep out of sight, except for occasional trips outside for air. Can was away most days on business. He never explained what he did and Fulya didn't ask, preferring not to know. He told her that Serkan Bey was concerned about Zeki's disappearance but had not interrogated him, leading him to believe that he was not under suspicion. Nevertheless, he was even more vigilant when he was out and about.

The previous evening he had returned with news. 'My father has told me that there will be another drug trafficking show at the restaurant tomorrow night. There wasn't one last week so Fatima and Gemma danced as usual. They think it went well with Gemma there which is why they've decided upon Wednesday again. Will you be up to doing it tomorrow?'

'Yes, I think so. The bruises and teeth marks have faded and you bought me a new outfit. I've been practising the dance moves which Fatima taught me, so hopefully everything will be OK.'

'Good, as long as you're up for it mentally,' Can said, an anxious look on his face.

'I've had a tough life, Can, and this has made me stronger, so *merak etme*.'

'All right then. We'll do the same as last time. I'll drop you in Taksim Square and you'll make your own way to the restaurant. You can change your clothes there. I'll tell Fatima not to come and hopefully Gemma will turn up. Remember – don't tell her anything about the drugs or Zeki Bey.'

'OK Can, you can trust me.'

*

Fulya pushed open the restaurant door and entered as confidently as she could, pleased that she had already been there and knew the layout. Mehmet Bey was sitting doing some paper work but rose to greet her. '*Merhaba*, Fatima,' he said, 'please sit down.' She had arrived early so there were no customers, only the waiter laying some tables. 'Tonight our special guests are coming so it will be the same routine as before; remember to lavish attention on them and give a five-star performance.'

'Of course, Mehmet Bey,' Fulya said, searching for any sign that Fatima's boss might have noticed something strange about her. She could see no hint of suspicion and felt herself relax. *This is going to be all right – just keep calm and enjoy yourself.* She went into her sister's room and began to prepare her face, using her twin's make-up. She brushed her hair until it shone, then changed into her new turquoise costume. She stood regarding her reflection critically, turning one way and then another. *Hmm, not bad. Hopefully I can pass as Fatima, inşallah.*

There was a knock on the door and in came Gemma. Fatima had phoned to warn her that Fulya would be dancing. '*Merhaba* Fulya,' she said, quickly adding, 'it's all right, Fatima's told me about the swap.'

'Oh! Thank goodness – I thought you'd seen through me,' Fulya said, her fright dissipating.

'It's OK. I must remember to call you "Fatima", that's all.' She quickly began to prepare herself as Fulya rummaged through her twin's costumes, holding them at arm's length.

'She has some lovely outfits,' she said.

'I'm sure she'd let you borrow some. She does with me.'

'I might do that the next time, that's if there is a next time.'

'Yes, it's a strange business, this stuffing heroin into your costume,' Gemma said, noting Fulya's look of consternation. 'Fatima thought I should know what's going on, but don't worry, I haven't told anyone.'

'You'd better not, especially Hasan. Is he here tonight?'

'Yes, he is, along with a friend, some guy he works with, I think. I'm sure Hasan's trustworthy, but I won't tell him.'

'You can't trust anyone in this game,' Fulya warned.

The signal came for them to dance and they entered together to loud clapping. Gemma began to move around the tables which seemed to be occupied by larger numbers of dodgy-looking men, while Fulya concentrated on the Mafia, trying not to focus on Zeki

Bey's absence. The glamourous Natalia sat at Serkan's side, draped in gold. Can gave her a knowing wink as she sank to the floor in front of him, spreading her legs wide. He slipped a sachet into her waistband, his warm hand soft on her skin. Next she approached the other two gangsters, who again were not accompanied by women. They both devoured her with their eyes as they furtively fumbled with her bodice, then waistband, pushing in more drugs. Lastly she focussed on Serkan Bey, feeling his close scrutiny, which sent a ripple of fear through her. 'You seem different tonight, Fatima,' he said, with a penetrating look.

'In what way, Sir?' she dared to ask.

'You are more assertive, more provocative, somehow. It's hard to explain.' He sat studying her closely, his hands together, as if in prayer.

'Maybe you are simply getting to know me better,' she replied, with a cheeky grin.

'Possibly,' he said, frowning.

Fulya danced away, glad to escape his unsettling remarks. *Can must be more like his mum,* she supposed. *He's so kind and considerate, unlike his dad – he gives me the creeps.* She approached a table near the door where a group of unsavoury-looking males were sitting smoking and drinking *rakı*. As she wiggled her hips at them she wondered if they were connected to Serkan's group, but they gave her nothing but stony stares.

Back in their dressing room in the break Fulya fished the drugs out of her clothes and locked them in the draw as Can had instructed. She was tempted to take a couple of sachets but knew that they'd be counted. *Don't be greedy – you've got a lot already,* she told herself, choosing to ignore the fact that she was reliant on Can to share the stash with her.

Gemma came in and sank down on the stool. 'That was some session,' she said, raising a bottle of water to her lips.

'It's certainly thirsty work. Did you get any tips from those nasty types by the door? They didn't give me any,' Fulya complained.

'No, all I got were frosty looks. It wouldn't have hurt them to smile.'

'I wonder if they're a rival group of criminals?'

'Who knows, Fulya. Let's just concentrate on the dancing.'

When they re-entered the restaurant, they noticed that the group of men had left. 'Thank goodness,' Fulya said in a low voice. 'We don't want mean types like that here.'

The rest of the evening passed without any problems, Fulya receiving more heroin and Gemma many tips. At the end Mehmet Bey carefully counted the sachets, congratulated Fulya on her performance and gave her an envelope full of notes. *I've certainly deceived him, but what about Serkan Bey?* she thought, wondering if he had said anything to Can. She said goodbye to Gemma, Hasan and his friend, who did not offer her a lift, this time believing her to be Fatima returning to Fatih by taxi.

Hasan drove over the Bosphorus Bridge, the floodlit mosques and lights from the Asian and European shores, along with numerous vessels bobbing on the waters below, a spectacular sight. 'What did you think of Fatima's dancing tonight?' Gemma asked, curious to know if he had noticed any difference.

'She was marvellous, but not quite as marvellous as before. There was something strange about her: I don't quite know what. Also she spent too long performing for those guys at the front again, and that Russian-looking woman. There's something weird going on there.'

'She was feeling a bit unwell tonight, that's all,' Gemma said quickly. 'And those men are friends of the owner,' she added, changing the subject hastily. Hasan dropped his friend off first and when he asked to come up to Gemma's flat she told him that she was too tired. 'I'll phone you,' she promised, kissing him on the cheek before he drove disappointedly away.

NINETEEN

Fulya huddled in the shadows of the shop doorway, wrapped up in her woollen coat and clutching a bag containing her costume. More than half-an-hour passed before Can appeared.

'*Çok özür dilerim,* I'm very sorry, Fulya, but my father insisted on speaking to me,' Can said, catching his breath.

'Was it something important?'

'Yes. I'll tell you about it in the car,' Can replied, holding her arm and hurrying towards his parked car. After the conversation with his dad his paranoia had increased dramatically.

He almost pushed Fulya into the front seat in his anxiety to get away and sped through the thinning late night traffic. Finally, when he reached the shore road he began to speak. 'My father is worried about the disappearance of Zeki Bey. He was asking me if I knew anything and of course I told him that I didn't, but I'm not sure that he believed me. I told you that he doesn't trust me and I'm certain he can detect if I'm lying.' He paused to light a cigarette, giving Fulya a worried glance.

'So what if he didn't believe you. What can he do? He wouldn't torture the information out of you, would he?'

'To be honest, Fulya, I don't know. He's never shown me much affection and he's ruthless – I wouldn't put anything past him.'

Fulya tossed her head as if to drive away his negativity. '*Merak etme.* Don't worry Can, I'm sure everything will be all right.'

'I wish I had your belief, but he was also suspicious of your behaviour. He might even suspect that you weren't Fatima.'

'He said something similar to me, but only about my manner, not my appearance. He won't know that Fatima has a twin because I was sent to Diyarbakır soon after my birth.'

'You don't know how powerful the Mafia are. He knows why Fatima came to Istanbul so he may know more about the family.'

'Why did she come here?'

'I think you should ask her that, Fulya. It's not for me to say.'

Can had been so upset when his father had told him about his darling's abusive uncle that he did not wish to think about it. He would gladly have travelled to the east and put a bullet through that evil man's head, but his father had cautioned him against it.

'OK, Can. I hope that I can meet my sister again soon.'

'I hope so too, but it's difficult. Tomorrow morning I have to phone my father – he did not say why. I am extremely uneasy about this. If anything were to happen to me you would be stuck on the yacht.'

'Oh, Can! I told you that I can swim, but he won't hurt you, I'm sure.'

'I hope that you are right,' Can said as he parked the Mercedes near the hidden dinghy. Soon they were safely on the yacht, but Can did not even feel secure there. Fulya went straight to bed but he sat smoking and drinking whisky into the small hours.

*

Can hung up the phone, his mouth dry and his head hammering. Serkan Bey had told him to be at the Pera Palace Hotel at two that afternoon. Fatima was to give them a private show, he had announced with a lewd laugh. Back in the Mercedes Can drank some water and rubbed some cologne into his temples. He felt sure that there was something sinister behind the planned performance and decided to phone Fatima: there was no reply.

At that moment Fatima was peering through the peephole of her apartment's front door. Two hefty-looking men were outside, hammering on it. 'Open up,' they were shouting, 'or we'll kick your door in.'

She opened it and they barged in, ignoring her cries of, 'who are you?'

'Get your belly dance costume. You're coming with us,' the heftier of the two commanded, watching as she bundled her turquoise outfit into a bag. She tried to resist as they pushed her outside but they flanked her, gripped her arms and propelled her down the stairs into a car with tinted windows. They parked near the Pera Palace and waited for the arrival of the Mafia. When Can drew up outside the famous hotel he was not in the mood to appreciate its beautiful nineteenth-century façade. He sat waiting for his father to appear and watched, with growing apprehension, as he got out of his Mercedes, Natalia on his arm and accompanied by the other two men. They were all wearing their black suits, grey shirts and black ties, their faces like masks, unmoving. He went over to them. 'It's good to see you' his father said, his eyes cold.

'What are we doing here?' Can queried.

'To have some fun,' his dad said and the other two men sniggered. They all entered the luxurious lobby and checked in. 'We're in Agatha Christie's room,' Serkan told Can.

'Why on earth?' Can asked.

'It's where she's supposed to have written, *Murder on the Orient Express*. Get it?' Can did not get it, but his father's mention of 'murder' made him feel sick with dread. They were ushered into the elevator and Can couldn't help admiring its beautifully polished wooden door and cast iron exterior as it gracefully ascended, despite his nerves. The attendant unlocked the door of room 411 and wished them a happy stay, after receiving a tip from Serkan Bey. They all piled in and lounged around waiting for Fatima, aware of the gold-painted, king-sized bed, covered with a burgundy and black bedspread, which dominated the room.

They did not have long to wait. Soon there was a knock at the door and Fatima entered with the two men, who were immediately dismissed by their boss. '*Hoş geldiniz*, Fatima,' Serkan Bey said, his voice like liquid toffee. Fatima said nothing, glowering at him, her dark eyes flashing. 'Where are your manners, Fatima? Be careful. Go and change into your costume and don't be long – we're waiting.' Fatima closed the bathroom door and locked it. The men fell silent and lit cigarettes while Natalia examined her face in the dressing-table mirror and applied some scarlet lipstick. Can wanted to say something to his father but the atmosphere was too tense. It was almost a relief to him when Fatima emerged from the bathroom, managing to look stunning in her costume with her face made up.

The men, except Can, clapped slowly while Natalia switched on a belly dance tape. Fatima began to dance, fixing her gaze first onto Serkan Bey's stern face, then Can's anxious one. The other two men were leering while Natalia chewed gum and tapped her feet in time with the music. The air was heavily laden with cigarette smoke, expensive after-shave and perfume and Fatima found it hard to breathe. Can watched her without pleasure, wondering what would happen next. 'Get closer to my men,' Can's dad ordered and Fatima obeyed.

'I am Devrim Bey,' the darker and hairier of the two said as he licked a lira note and stuck it on her forehead.

Fatima gave a slight bow and approached the second pale, smooth-faced man, gyrating her hips towards him. 'My name's Zafer,' he said, tucking a note into her waistband, his fingers lingering.

Devrim and Zafer – Revolution and Victory: such glorious names, but they are not living up to them, Can thought, wishing that he could intervene as his father commanded his love to come next to him. Fatima glided over to Serkan Bey, her eyes full of fear. As he slid a note into her top he stared directly at her and suddenly snapped, 'What do you know about Zeki Bey's disappearance?'

Can sat up straight his mind racing. *So this is what this is all about,* he realised, horribly aware that he was to blame. Fatima had stopped dancing. She stood uncertainly in front of the Mafia boss and asked, 'Who is Zeki Bey?'

'The other one of my men, as if you didn't know.'

Serkan's eyes bored into Fatima's. She resolutely returned his gaze and stated, 'I did not know his name, nor that he was missing.'

'You didn't notice that he wasn't there last night?'

Fatima briefly turned to look at Can. *She needs my help, but I am powerless,* he moaned to himself. 'I did see that there were only four of you, plus Natalia, of course,' Fatima said, with a glance at the Russian, who remained silent.

'Zeki has been missing for a week. You were behaving strangely last night. Why was that, Fatima?'

Once again she glanced at Can but could tell nothing from his return look. 'I was feeling a bit ill, that's all.'

Abruptly, Serkan turned to his son and barked, 'And what about you?'

Can's feeling of disquiet increased dramatically, his mouth almost too dry to speak. 'What about me?' he managed, knowing that this would only anger his father.

'Don't play games with me, son. I've seen her looking at you and how you look at her. You're in this together, aren't you?'

'I don't know what you mean, Father.'

'OK, if you want to be like that, we'll let the guys have some fun,' Serkan said with a lewd look at his men.

Before Can could say anything Fatima spoke. 'I'm afraid it is the wrong time of the month for me to have fun, as you say. This is why I felt unwell last night.'

'Ugh! You have an answer for everything, young lady, but your mouth is not bleeding, I think.' Serkan regarded Fatima's pale face dispassionately. 'Start dancing,' he ordered.

'Please don't humiliate her,' Can pleaded.

'Just tell us what you did with Zeki and we'll stop.' Can did not trust himself to speak, knowing that his father would see through any lies. 'Your silence is deafening, son. This woman has already been humiliated. She is spoiled goods. We can do anything to her. Begin!'

Fatima stood motionless. 'Begin!' Serkan shouted, pulling a pistol from his pocket.

She had no choice and began dancing to the music, edging closer to the two men who were devouring her with their eyes. Zafer was the first to reveal his stiff member. He grabbed her by the hair and forced her head down. 'Suck it, you bitch,' he groaned and she complied as his thrusts became faster and faster until he came, forcing her to gag. He released her and she stood up, wiping her mouth.

'Bravo, my dear, but you should learn to swallow it – it's very nutritious,' Serkan said, covering Natalia's hand which was gripping his own erection inside his trousers.

Throughout Fatima's ordeal Can had felt compelled to watch, his emotions a mixture of disgust, lust and compassion. At times he had imagined himself as the recipient, but when he became aroused he was revolted both at himself and Zafer, lastly feeling full of compassion for his darling. He regarded his father with horror, hardly believing that they had the same blood. 'Let's stop this now,' he said, looking beseechingly at his dad.

'Don't you want to feel her lovely tongue, Can?'

'Why, you. . .' Can lunged at Serkan who pushed him back in his chair.

'Be careful, my son. I've told you already, just tell us what's happened to our friend and this will stop.'

'I can't answer that question.'

'Can't or won't?' Serkan said menacingly. When he received no reply he again commanded Fatima to dance. Before she began she fixed Can with a look so cold it froze his being. *She will never love me now,* he thought, full of despair.

Once more Fatima danced and once more she was subjected to the same ordeal, this time with Devrim Bey. Zafer had pleasured himself again while watching and Natalia had brought her own lovely lips down on Serkan Bey's huge erection. Can simply sat observing their carnal behaviour, trying to distance himself from the proceedings, his mind numb. Fatima retreated into the bathroom while the men recovered from their orgasms to the sound of water splashing and gargling. She emerged looking remarkably calm after her foul experience. 'May I leave now?' she asked Serkan.

'I'll get the same men to drive you home. They're waiting in the lobby.'

'I can drive her,' Can said.

'I'm sure you'd love to, Can, but you're coming with us,' Serkan said, a ghastly expression on his face. Can felt sick and gazed hopelessly at his love, fearing it might be for the last time.

*

Natalia escorted Fatima down in the lift first, handing her over to the waiting men. Can was squashed into the elevator with the others and they emerged together from the hotel's entrance into the gathering gloom. They stood briefly in the brightly lit car park. Suddenly a shot pierced the night and they glimpsed a black car speeding away, the front passenger window being rapidly raised. Devrim Bey slumped to the ground, clutching his chest. 'They've shot me,' he groaned, blood beginning to spread across his shirt.

Several people, including the doorman, ran out. Serkan Bey immediately took charge. 'It's all right, he's a friend of ours. We'll take him to hospital,' he said, telling Zafer and Can to lift him up. He quickly brought their car, and, ignoring the protestations of the hotel's staff, they bundled Devrim onto the back seat and drove away.

Can and Zafer sat on either side of him. Can felt his wrist. 'I think he might be dead,' he announced, 'I can't feel his pulse.'

'If that's so we'll have to get rid of the body – we don't want the police involved,' Serkan said, briefly turning his head.

Can saw his chance. 'Maybe this is what happened to Zeki Bey?'

'You could be right, Can. There was a group of our rivals at the restaurant last night, sitting by the door. I was wondering why they were there. I think they've discovered about the drug trafficking and belly dancing and they want a piece of the action. I suspected that Zeki was doing some independent dealing and he would have been carrying a lot of heroin – worth being murdered for.'

'That sounds about right,' Can said, inwardly breathing a sigh of relief.

'We'll worry about who did it later. How about burying him in Eyüp Cemetery?' Serkan suggested.

'That's a long way,' Can complained.

'I know but I want our dear friend to have a peaceful resting place and the cemetery's so large we're bound to find a vacant piece of ground,' his father said.

'I'm not so sure. I've been there and it's full of graves of famous people,' Zafer added.

'I'll drive there any way and we'll see,' Serkan said with such authority that no more arguments were raised. He drove along beside the Golden Horn towards the cemetery, which was on the steep slope of a hill at the end of it. It was late by the time they got there and very dark. Serkan parked the car near the top of the cemetery and turned off the headlights. The three men and Natalia peered through the windows at the Ottoman-style tombs which spread dark shadows on the ground. It was a cloudy night, partly obscuring a half-moon and the hoot of an owl made them all jump.

'It's a bit spooky, isn't it? I'm going to stay right here,' Natalia stated, clutching at the collar of her fur coat.

'That's OK. We can take care of this,' Serkan replied, getting out of the car and rummaging in the boot for shovels and pick axes. Can and Zafer followed, looking around apprehensively.

'We'll need to bury him here, at the edge. He's too heavy to carry,' Can remarked.

'All right, let's get digging,' Serkan commanded and they began, soon abandoning their coats, their laboured breathing sounding strange, surrounded by skeletons.

Can paused to wipe away the sweat from his forehead. 'This ground's so hard and stony. I doubt if we can dig deep enough.'

'Just keep digging. It has to be deep enough to cover him, at least,' Serkan replied, putting on his leather gloves to protect his soft hands from blisters: he generally ordered other people to do the hard work. Eventually they had dug a shallow grave and stood, leaning on their shovels surveying their handiwork.

'Do you think that's enough?' Zafer asked, lighting a cigarette.

'It'll have to be,' Serkan said. He was exhausted by the unexpected exertion. 'I'll just make sure he's dead,' he said, opening the car's back door. He felt Devrim's pulse and listened hard for any breathing. The body was beginning to smell, turning his stomach. 'Let's get him out of here,' he said, emerging from the car and standing back. Zafer grabbed the body's legs and pulled him out onto the ground. Natalia watched, pressing a perfumed handkerchief to her nose. Can took hold of his head and between them they carried him to the grave and laid him to rest. The three men stood, heads bowed, while Serkan muttered a short prayer, then they quickly shovelled the earth and stones back onto the body. He was hardly covered by the time they had finished and each thought, but did not say, that wild dogs would find the corpse and dig it up. Like Zeki, Devrim had not been married and if the police were to be alerted and investigated his identity, they would have seen his name on their records as being one of the Mafia and would have closed the case.

They placed the tools back in the boot and got into the car, Can and Zafer trying to avoid sitting on the back seat's mess. Serkan drove off down the hill again, the city's lights spread out below them.

'I need to get back to my car,' Can said, thinking that Fulya would be worried about him.

'I don't want to go near the Pera Palace, just in case,' said his father. 'I'll have to drop you nearby.'

'OK,' said Can, not wishing to antagonise him. He hoped that his dad had dismissed the idea that he was responsible for Zeki's disappearance. They reached the hotel environs with no further incident and Can found his car. It was well past midnight, the streets quiet except for a few stray cats and dogs who were foraging for food in the rubbish. When he reached the yacht there was no sign of Fulya. *Good. She must have gone to bed,* he thought with relief, pouring himself a whisky before he washed the grime from his body.

TWENTY

A thick fog shrouded the sea when Fulya awoke. She lay in bed listening to the ships' horns booming, wondering if Can had returned. She had waited until after midnight for him, then had gone to sleep, unable to keep her eyes open. She slipped out of bed, put on her dressing gown and padded into the saloon. The empty whisky decanter and overflowing ashtray told her all she needed to know. She had a soothing shower, dressed in her casual clothes and went to the kitchen to make coffee and prepare breakfast. She had got used to living on the yacht but yearned to have a life on land again. The aroma of fresh coffee brewing must have woken Can and he appeared in the doorway, his hair tousled, his eyes red-rimmed, a dark shadow of stubble on his chin. '*Günaydın.* Good morning, Can,' Fulya said, flashing him a bright smile.

'*Günaydın,* Fulya,' Can replied, his voice croaking.

'Have you caught a cold?' Fulya asked, feeling concern for her host: she still did not regard him as a friend.

Can sat on a stool at the counter and poured himself some coffee. He took a couple of mouthfuls before replying. 'I had a hard night,' he said, examining his blistered hands.

'What have you been doing?' Fulya sat silently as he told her about the hotel meeting, omitting to mention Fatima and his father's suspicions, then describing Devrim's shooting and the disposal of his body.

'Good God, how terrible! No wonder you look shattered,' she said, wondering if he had told her the whole story. *Two men down and three to go,* she thought.

'I'm going to take it easy on the yacht today,' Can said.

'That seems like a good idea. The police won't think of looking for you here.'

'It's not the police I'm worried about.' Can scowled into his coffee cup.

Fulya decided to change the subject. 'I would really like to meet my sister again, Can: I've got so many questions to ask her. Could you phone her and arrange a meeting somewhere when you're next off the boat?'

Can sighed deeply before replying, making her ponder if it were related to Fatima. Eventually he said, 'All right, I'll do that, but I think she should come here – it'll be safer that way.'

Fulya was so happy at the prospect of seeing her twin again that she did not press for anything else.

*

Can was as good as his word and phoned Fatima the next day. It was a difficult conversation: she gave monosyllabic responses to his apologies until he mentioned Fulya's desire to meet. Then she agreed for him to take her to the yacht. 'I can come on Monday as I'm not working,' she said and Can arranged to pick her up from her flat, a small spark of hope igniting in his heart.

On Monday morning after Can had left Fulya continued with her cleaning of the yacht. With time on her hands she had been methodically giving the boat an early spring clean, and, as the weather was dry and calm, she decided to sweep and then polish the front deck. As she was standing surveying the burnished boards she heard the splash of oars and looked over the side. '*Hoş geldiniz,*' she cried to Can and Fatima.

'*Hoş bulduk,*' her twin answered before she clambered up the ladder, kissed Fulya on both cheeks and then hugged her. They released each other, ignoring Can who had been carrying food supplies into the kitchen. Fulya noticed her sister's pale face, her tired eyes and her lack of make-up, aware that her own appearance was healthily vibrant by comparison. Suddenly they felt a few heavy drops of rain and hurried inside.

'Oh, my lovely polished deck will be getting all wet,' Fulya moaned.

'You have been busy,' Fatima said looking around the immaculate saloon.

'Yes, well, I need to do something active, being stuck on here all day.'

'Does Can never take you anywhere?' Fatima nodded towards the kitchen and raised her eyebrows.

'No, he's too busy and he's scared to be seen with me.'

'Why is that?'

'He doesn't want Serkan Bey's lot to know that there are two of us because that would put us in danger, especially you.'

Fatima began to twist a strand of her hair. 'Hey, let's not dwell on this. I've got so much to ask you,' Fulya said.

Can appeared carrying two glasses of *çay* and a plate of sweet pastries on a silver tray. 'Oh, Can, *çok teşekkür ederiz.* I've been so busy with my sister I haven't done anything to help.'

'That's all right, Fulya. I know you two have lots to talk about so I'll leave you to it.' He gave Fatima a weak smile which she returned with little warmth.

Once he had gone Fulya asked, 'What's with you two?'

'Something happened but I don't want to discuss it,' Fatima said, twisting her hair tighter.

'If there's something wrong, you must tell me.'

Fatima stared at her twin and knew that she was right – they could not keep anything secret from each other. Hesitantly at first and then with increasing anger, she told Fulya everything that had happened in the Pera Palace's room. Fulya had listened silently and once her twin had finished she held out her arms and let her sob and sob. Once Fatima's crying had ceased she added her own news of Devrim's shooting and subsequent burial. 'You'll be glad that one of those monsters has been blown away,' she said grimly.

'He may have been a monster, Fulya, but he was from God and I pray that his soul has found peace,' Fatima said, bowing her head and uttering a small prayer.

Fulya was astonished at her sister's forgiving nature. 'How can you say that after what he made you do?'

'Simply because I can, *canım.* If I had not forgiven those who had violated me in my life, I would now be like a worm-infested apple – rotten to the core.'

'Oh, how I wish that I could be as good as you, dear Fatima. I would kill every one of those soldiers who raped me in a back alley in Diyarbakır, if I were able to,' Fulya said, her face twisted in anger.

'Oh, Fulya, how terrible!' It was Fatima's turn to hold her twin as she shook with angry tears in her arms. When Fulya was calm again she asked, 'So is that why you came to Istanbul?'

'Yes. The distant relations who had brought me up found out and banished me from their house. I had a little money and used it to buy a bus ticket to Istanbul. You know the rest.'

Fatima nodded and then shared her own reason for leaving the east. They cried some more and comforted each other, listening to the sound of hail pounding on the roof.

*

The twins had been so immersed in their conversation that they had not heard a speedboat's engine. Its captain had tied it up and ascended the ladder where he was accosted by Can. 'Zafer Bey! What are you doing here?'

'Thanks for your kind greetings, Can,' Zafer said sarcastically, his waterproofs dripping wet after the hail storm. 'Your father has sent me to find out what you're up to.'

'This is preposterous – what does he think I'm up to?'

'He's not sure but I guess he's wondering if Zeki Bey was here.'

'And why would he be with me?'

'I don't know but maybe he thinks that you are drug trafficking together and this is a good place to hide.'

'Not so good if you know where I am. It's ridiculous.'

'Well, now I'm here why don't you be a gracious host and invite me in? I'm wet and cold and would welcome a glass of something warming.' The storm had passed but a bitter wind was blowing.

Can reluctantly ushered his unwanted guest inside, hoping that the twins would have heard their voices and hidden in their rooms. It was not to be. Zafer gasped when he saw them sitting close together on the settee. 'What magic is this? Am I really seeing two Fatimas?' He looked from one to the other, his mouth agape.

'Good afternoon, Zafer Bey,' Fulya said, her voice sharp as glass.

'*Iyi günler* to you too, Fatima, that's if you are her,' Zafer replied, regaining his composure and remembering the reason for his visit. 'Please show me the rest of the yacht, Can.'

'Follow me,' said Can, leading the way to his room, the bathroom and the guest rooms.

Zafer whistled when he saw that they were both occupied, Fulya's nightdress on the bed, her make-up on the dressing table and Fatima's bag in the other room. 'You lucky devil! You've got both these lovelies here all to yourself, Can. No wonder you didn't want to participate last Thursday.'

'It's not what it looks like, Zafer. Anyway, I hope you are satisfied that I am not hiding Zeki Bey.'

'He's not inside, certainly, but I think I should check outside,' Zafer said, going out onto the deck.

Can let him go, content to remain in the warmth of the saloon. He was about to speak to the twins when they heard a loud thump. They all rushed out and saw Zafer slumped on the front deck, a thin stream of blood trickling from his head. 'Oh! He must have slipped on my polished wood,' Fulya said, a slow smile lighting up her face.

Can cautiously approached his prostrate form, careful not to fall himself. 'He's still breathing,' he assured the sisters.

Fulya was not, however, assured. 'That's too bad. Let's kill him now then throw him into the sea, like Zeki Bey.'

'What do you mean, "like Zeki Bey,"?' Fatima asked.

Can and Fulya exchanged a worried look. 'I'm sorry, Can,' Fulya said, then to Fatima, 'I'll explain later, sis, but we didn't murder him, honest.'

'OK, you can tell me later but what about Zafer, you just said you want to dispose of him.'

'Surely you do too after what he made you do,' Fulya said in exasperation.

'No, I don't, Fulya. Zafer Bey is also from God, like Devrim Bey and all other beings.'

'Girls,' Can interrupted, 'you must postpone the God debate. Right now we need to get Zafer inside out of the cold. Please help me.'

Fulya grimaced but bent to help lift his heavy body which they carried into the lounge and lay on the floor. Can searched for his gun and removed it. Fatima brought a wet towel and carefully cleaned the gash on his head. The blood had stopped flowing and the wound was not as deep as she had thought. Colour began to return to his cheeks and then his eyes opened. 'What happened to me?' he asked, staring up into Fatima's dark eyes.

'You slipped and fell on the deck.'

'Are you certain you didn't push me?'

'No-one pushed you. If we'd wanted to get rid of you would we be helping you now?' Can said, giving Fulya a stern stare.

Zafer groaned and tried to sit up. Fatima put her arms under his shoulders and heaved him up so that his back was resting on the sofa. 'That's better, thanks Fatima.'

'I think you should stay here for tonight, Zafer. It's getting dark and you might be concussed,' Can said. Fulya gave an even bigger grimace while Fatima's face was impassive.

'That's kind of you Can,' Zafer said, without a trace of sarcasm.

'That's OK. You can sleep on the settee. It converts into a bed.'

'So, I'm not invited to join in your cosy threesome,' Zafer quipped, receiving no response from Can or the twins.

He searched for his gun and Can said, 'I've taken your gun as a precaution.'

'Will I get it back?'

'No,' Can said and Zafer sat in sulky silence.

That night they all slept uneasily, their doors locked, listening for the slightest sound from their unwanted guest. The morning dawned bright and sunny, the air clear after the storm. Zafer left and as he descended the ladder he shouted up to Can and the twins, 'I'll have to tell Serkan Bey about this.'

'Tell him, what do I care,' Can shouted back.

TWENTY-ONE

Gemma was worried. She had not heard from Fatima since their last dance two weeks earlier and it had been nearly three weeks since their night in Kadiköy. She had tried phoning but there was no reply. Now it was another Wednesday and she had decided to go to the restaurant. Hasan and his friend Ali were also keen to go and, despite Gemma's longing to spend another night with Fatima, she had agreed to be accompanied by them. She would feel safer with two strong men, she reasoned.

It was Gemma's fifth time of performing so her nervousness as she entered the restaurant was not connected with that; no, it was because of Fatima. Would it be her or Fulya dancing? What had happened to her beloved? Was she safe? These questions buzzed around in her head until Fatima, or was it Fulya, came to greet her, Hasan and Ali. '*Hoş geldiniz,*' she said with a warm smile, kissing Gemma slowly on both cheeks. *Yes, it's her – I'd recognise that divine smell anywhere,* Gemma thought, her heart feeling lighter. She quickly followed her friend into the changing room, leaving Hasan and Ali sitting at a table near the door.

Once inside they embraced, holding each other as time stood still. Reluctantly they drew apart. 'I've been trying to phone you,' Gemma complained.

'I'm so sorry, Gemma but a lot has happened. We'll meet up soon, I promise,' Fatima said, her dark eyes unfathomable. Gemma had to be content with this and began to get ready, putting on the scarlet outfit. Fatima dressed in an emerald green one, the colour of Islam, Gemma noted. She also noticed Fatima reciting what sounded like a prayer under her breath, at the same time fingering the blue evil eye amulet hanging above her mirror.

There was a knock at the door and Mehmet came in, his face anxious and drawn. '*İyi geceler,* girls. Our special guests may come tonight but there might be less of them,' he said, staring at Fatima.

'And why is that?' Fatima asked innocently.

'I'm not sure,' Mehmet replied.

He's obviously hiding something, Gemma thought, trying not to look interested.

'OK. I'll knock on the door as usual and you can go in first, Fatima.'

As soon as he had gone Gemma hissed, 'Do you know what's happened to some of the Mafia, Fatima?'

'Yes, I do but I can't say anything here, Gemma.'

'All right, but you'd better tell me soon.' Fatima nodded then jumped up as the door was knocked. She hurried out without a backward glance leaving Gemma to wonder what had happened.

Serkan Bey, Natalia, Zafer and Can were all sitting in the front again, dressed in their black suits, Natalia in a black evening dress. The restaurant was full, the air heavy with cigarette smoke, mingled with perfume, after-shave and fried fish. Fatima began to dance in the centre of the stage then started to work the tables, initially avoiding the Mafia. She could hardly bear to look at them, especially Zafer Bey. Eventually though she approached them and Serkan Bey said in a low voice, 'Don't ignore us, Fatima, or are you her double?' as he slipped a packet into her bodice. Fatima simply smiled and moved towards Can whose eyes bored into hers as he also slid some drugs into her bra.

Gemma came out onto the floor to more loud applause and began circulating receiving many tips. She noticed that Hasan and Ali were not watching the dancing – they were watching the door. Fatima was performing on the floor in front of the special guests, her legs spread wide, her arms high above her head, fingers entwined, when the door burst open. Several armed policemen charged in and went straight towards the group of Mafia, quickly handcuffing the men and removing their guns, at the same time holding Natalia and Fatima.

The music still played but the customers sat in shocked silence while Gemma stood motionless, watching a policeman gripping her darling's arm. Mehmet Bey, who had been hiding behind the bar, was the next to be arrested. One of the police, who appeared to be the chief, addressed the room. 'Don't anyone move until we have left,' he ordered and then jerked his head towards the others who marched the four men and two women briskly out of the door into a waiting police vehicle. Soon they drove away and slowly the restaurant came back to life, the waiters circulating, dealing with customers anxious to pay their bills and escape the place. Others chatted excitedly, wondering what the black-suited men had done and what the relationship was between the Turkish belly dancer, the beautiful blonde lady and them.

Hasan went over to Gemma, who was still standing in the same position, and led her into the changing room where she sank down on the stool. Her face was pale, her body icy cold. 'I'll get you some water and something stronger,' Hasan said, quickly returning with a bottle and a glass of whisky.

Gemma took a sip of water and managed a weak smile. 'Drink some of this. It'll warm you up,' Hasan urged and she drank some, pulling a face.

'I don't like whisky,' she said, but some colour was returning to her cheeks. Hasan waited for her to say more, expecting her to question the arrests, but instead she asked, 'Why didn't they arrest me?'

'Why should they have? You weren't doing anything wrong, were you?'

Gemma stared hard at him. He didn't seem to be shocked, in fact, he seemed to be calm, almost as if he had been expecting the police. Then she remembered: he had not been watching her dancing, he had been watching the door, along with Ali. 'You knew they were coming, didn't you?'

'Yes. My uncle is a chief in the drugs squad. It was him who took charge,' Hasan admitted.

'But how did you know there was anything wrong?'

'Simply by observing their behaviour. Fatima spent a lot of time with them and I could see that they were putting something larger than a note in her costume.'

'Oh, I see. I didn't think anybody would notice.'

'What are you saying, Gemma? You knew what was going on?'

'Yes, Fatima told me. She was forced into it, Hasan. You have to get her out.'

'What makes you so sure that she's innocent?'

'Because I know her. The Mafia knew about her background and if she hadn't complied, they would have told everyone and ruined her life.'

'I see. Well, it's in the hands of the police now.'

'But they may do terrible things to her. Please ask your uncle to use his influence.'

Hasan wanted to impress Gemma. 'I will see what I can do,' he promised.

*

Hasan drove Gemma and Ali back to Kadıköy, there was nothing he could do that night, he had persuaded Gemma. He would phone his uncle in the morning. Gemma's sleep was disturbed by images of Fatima imprisoned in a tiny cell, or worse, being tortured or abused, pictures from the film, *Midnight Express*, flashing through her mind. She was glad that it was her day off and towards dawn she fell into a deep slumber.

'Good morning, or should I say afternoon,' Tina greeted her when she finally surfaced. Gemma craved a quiet breakfast but was forced to answer Tina's questions. 'Wow, that's some exciting night you've had. I guess you won't be dancing there again?'

Gemma hadn't thought about her dancing, she was too concerned about Fatima. 'I suppose you're right, Tina; with Mehmet Bey in jail I don't know what will happen to the restaurant, but I'm only thinking about Fatima right now.' She had just finished eating when the phone rang. 'That'll be for me,' she told Tina, jumping up and rushing into the lounge.

Hasan's voice sounded strange. 'Hello, Gemma. I've spoken to my uncle and he will try to get Fatima released but it's not that easy, they may want to put her on trial first.'

'Oh, that's too bad, Hasan,' Gemma said, declining his offer to come round and cheer her up. Only Fatima's release could end her gloominess. She went back in the kitchen and told Tina the bad news.

'Try not to worry, Gemma. You know how things work here – a bit of baksheesh works wonders. In fact they probably found loads of money and drugs on them so they'll be well happy.'

'I hope you're right, Tina. There's something else that's worrying me. Fulya's stranded on the yacht now and I should go and get her, but I'm not too keen on going alone.'

'Fulya? Who's Fulya?'

'Oh, sorry Tina, I'd forgotten that you didn't know about Fulya.' As quickly as she could Gemma told Tina about Fatima's twin, Can and the yacht, as well as the dancing.

'That's some story, Gemma. Why can't you go with Hasan to the yacht?'

'I don't trust him now. He could arrange to get Fulya arrested too.'

'Hmm. I suppose you're right. I guess I could go with you, but when? There's no time today because it'll soon be dark and we're teaching in the morning.'

'How about Saturday afternoon, directly after our morning lessons have finished?'

'I guess that's just about doable,' Tina said.

*

At midday on Saturday Gemma and Tina hurried out of school to catch a ferry from Kadıköy to Beşiktaş, on the European shore. From there they boarded a crowded bus which crawled along the traffic-clogged road beside the Bosphorus. Fatima had told Gemma where the yacht was moored, but it was difficult to locate the turn off, especially as she had to peer around people's heads to see out of the window. At length they reached Bebek, and got off the bus.

Tina looked at the fine yachts and splendid Ottoman-style mansions. 'This is some high-class place.'

'Yes, isn't it. I wish we had time to explore but we must go back down the road and look for a side turning.' The girls started walking and after about half-an-hour they found a track. 'I hope this is it,' Gemma said as they began to walk faster, aware that it was getting late. At the end was the sea, and to their relief a luxury yacht was anchored offshore. 'Now to find the dinghy,' Gemma said, beginning to search the shoreline. 'Let's look under those bushes,' she told Tina and soon they had uncovered the dinghy. They dragged it out away from the undergrowth and into the sea, getting their feet wet. Once in they grabbed an oar each and, after a few minutes of uncoordinated rowing, began to move smoothly over the sea, which was calm, the weather dry.

As they drew up alongside the vessel Fulya appeared, recognised Gemma and shouted, 'Am I glad to see you – I thought I was going to have to swim ashore if someone hadn't come soon.'

Gemma and then Tina clambered up the ladder. Fulya hugged them both in turn, after Gemma had introduced Tina, and took them into the saloon where they both stood admiring the sumptuous décor and furnishings. There was, however, little time to linger as darkness would soon be descending, so they quickly told Fulya about the arrests. 'That's awful – we must do something,' she cried.

'Hasan is trying to get Fatima released,' Gemma said.

'Yes, but what about Can? He's not really one of them – he's such a good person,' Fulya said.

'I don't know what we can do about Can, Fulya, but for now what would you like to do? You could come home with us, couldn't she, Tina?'

'For one or two nights, but not for longer. It's forbidden to share our flat because it belongs to the school we teach at,' Tina explained.

'That's OK. I'm dying to get off this boat, even if it's only for a couple of days.' That being agreed she rapidly put some clothes and other essentials into a bag, locked the doors and joined the girls in the dinghy.

It was getting dark by the time they found a bus stop and once more had to squash themselves onto a crowded bus. The ferry was equally busy with people returning home after their Saturday excursions and the three of them sighed with relief when they finally reached Kadıköy. 'I'm starving,' Tina announced outside the terminal and the others agreed. There had been no time to eat.

'Let's go for a big meal. I've got some money,' Fulya said, feeling Zeki Bey's notes in her pocket.

'It's OK, Fulya, we can pay for ourselves,' Gemma said, thinking that she was feeling embarrassed about her lack of money.

'No, really, I have money and I want to pay for you,' Fulya insisted. Gemma decided not to argue and they headed to one of the central restaurants where they stuffed themselves with *meze* and kebabs, washed down with a bottle of red wine. They had been too busy eating and drinking to chat but as soon as they'd finished Fulya began to wonder about Fatima and Can. 'Maybe I can go to the police station,' she suggested.

'I don't think that's a good idea – they might arrest you too,' Gemma said, continuing, 'we must wait and see what Hasan can do tomorrow.' Fulya reluctantly agreed and they went to the flat where Gemma made up the settee with bedding, wishing that Fulya was Fatima.

TWENTY-TWO

Gemma and Tina left Fulya sleeping while they went to their Sunday morning classes. At noon Hasan was waiting for Gemma outside. Tina had accompanied her and hovered, hoping for some news. 'Have you heard anything about Fatima? It's all right, Tina knows,' Gemma told him.

'Yes, I have good news. Fatima will be released today, God willing,' Hasan said with a broad smile.

'Oh, that's wonderful! How did you manage that?' Gemma asked.

'I don't know exactly but my uncle would have told them that she had been forced to do it.'

'I bet baksheesh was involved,' Tina interrupted.

'Possibly. Unfortunately, this is how our country operates quite often, but in this case it has produced a good result, don't you think?'

'Yes, of course it has,' Gemma said, her eyes shining. Hasan wanted to take her for lunch so she agreed even though she wanted to phone Fatima. The meal seemed to last forever and when he suggested returning together to her flat she told him that she was too tired. 'I'll phone you,' she promised. She could not risk him seeing Fulya.

Fulya was sitting watching television when she arrived home. She immediately jumped up in excitement when she saw the huge grin on Gemma's face. 'She's been released, hasn't she?' she asked, then hugged Gemma hard when she heard the news. 'We must try and phone her.'

'Yes, I'll do that right now,' Gemma said, picking up the phone and dialling. It rang and rang, continuing all evening until finally they gave up and went to bed, to dream anxiously about Fatima.

The next day Gemma came home from work at lunchtime and found a note from Fulya. *Fatima is home and I have gone to stay with her*, she read. She immediately dialled Fatima's number and was thrilled to hear her voice. 'Thank goodness you are free,' she said.

'*Merhaba*, Gemma. Yes, I am so glad to be home. It was awful in jail. Fulya is coming soon and I'm not certain what she will do now with Can locked up.'

'No, it's difficult for her. And what about you? With Mehmet Bey arrested will you still have a job?'

'This I also don't know, Gemma. I have tried phoning the restaurant but there is no reply. I may go there on Wednesday to see what's happening.'

'Maybe we could meet then? I want to see you so much.'

'I'm not sure what time I'll be there or if Fulya will still be with me. I'll phone you that evening and we can arrange a meeting.' Gemma had to be satisfied with her response and hoped that things would work out for the twins.

*

On Wednesday evening Fatima called Gemma as promised. '*Iyi geceler*, Gemma. I went to the restaurant today but it was locked, with a 'Closed until further notice' sign on the door. Fulya is still staying with me and we are going to start looking for other belly dancing jobs. We might even get one together,' she said with a chuckle.

'That would certainly be unusual,' Gemma said.

'It would be, wouldn't it? We are going to be busy but Ramadan begins next Tuesday and I want to visit Hudai's tomb in Üsküdar again. Would you like to come with us next Wednesday?'

This was Gemma's first holy month of Ramadan and she was looking forward to it with mixed feelings. Her Turkish friends had assured her that food would be readily available all day, with restaurants and cafés open, but she was still concerned about eating and drinking in public. Outside of the big cities it was a different situation with most people fasting from sunrise to sunset and eating places closed until the fast ended. 'I would like to come with you, Fatima, but will you be fasting?'

'Yes, I will be but I don't know about Fulya. Anyway, that's not a problem – you may eat in front of me, I don't mind.'

'That's sweet of you, Fatima, but I will try not to. At least now in February it must be easier to fast than in the summer with its long, hot days.'

'Yes, that's true. We'll meet you at the Üsküdar ferry terminal around two, if that's all right?'

'Yes, fine, I'll see you there.' Gemma put the phone down wishing that it was next Wednesday already.

*

On the first day of Ramadan Gemma awoke in the pre-dawn darkness to the rhythmic beating of a drum. The sound became louder and louder, then faded away as the drummer left her street. She lay awake thinking of Fatima getting up and eating breakfast before the sun rose. She drifted off but was woken again by the muezzin's call to prayer. She had grown used to hearing the call five times a day but it seemed to be especially strident in Ramadan at sunrise and sunset. She felt tired all day after this early awakening and her students were sleepy and difficult to teach. 'It will get easier as the month progresses,' one of them assured her. As she hurried home in the late afternoon there was a distinct buzz of anticipation amongst the crowds, many of whom were queueing outside the baker's shop for their special Ramadan large, round flat breads, their tops sprinkled with sesame and black Nigella seeds. Mainly head-scarfed women wearing ankle-length coats and bleary-eyed men, their faces dark with a shadow of black stubble were standing patiently waiting. She joined a line, lured by the appetising smell and general feeling of togetherness, imagining that she was also about to break her fast. After the evening prayer families and friends met and ate special food together for most of the evening. Gemma felt the pull of this devotedness, something which her life had lacked, and which may have drawn her to a Moslem country where hospitality to strangers was a part of the religion.

The next day she squashed into a *dolmuş*, which literally means 'stuffed': a shared taxi which only goes when it is full. Many of these vehicles were ancient American cars, similar to the iconic ones used in Havana. She got out in Üsküdar and made her way to the ferry terminal, avoiding the persistent shoe-shine boys, who constantly made her laugh with their attempts to shine her shoes, even when she was wearing trainers. Fatima and Fulya were waiting for her, wearing matching navy blue headscarves and dark-coloured clothes, their faces free of make-up. They greeted each other warmly with kisses on both cheeks, then crossed the busy road, passed numerous small shops selling jewellery and other goods until they reached the steep street up to the tomb. Gemma put on her black headscarf, carefully covering all her hair, as they approached the steps up to Hudai's resting place. Gemma paused to read the inscription, then followed the twins. There was a small, silent queue outside the tomb of mainly mature women, well wrapped up against the chilly air, which the girls joined. The line moved slowly forward until they were inside. Gemma noticed a cat, this time a tabby one, tightly curled up in a dark corner, his head on his paws. She felt awed by the huge tomb which was covered with a dark green cloth on which were swirls of Arabic lettering. It was enclosed by an ornate golden grill and the high ceiling was surrounded by a black frieze with gold calligraphy. The atmosphere of total devotion affected Gemma deeply and she shut her eyes, clinging tightly onto the grill. When she came to the tomb, like Fatima and Fulya, she lay her forehead upon it and silently prayed for an end to war, a peaceful feeling permeating her body. She sensed that the twins were both praying for the speedy release of Can and Mehmet Bey, subtly connected to each other. They each moved away from the tomb but stayed, leaning against the wall, reluctant to leave. Eventually, as if propelled by a common impulse, they slowly went outside and sat on a bench in the late afternoon sunshine. Still affected by Hudai's presence they remained silent for a while, then looked at each other and smiled. *I shall treasure this moment forever*, Gemma thought.

TWENTY-THREE

Ramadan had ended and spring was in the air. The streets were filled with stray kittens, buds were about to burst open on the cherry trees while flower sellers displayed the first daffodils and barrows piled high with strawberries appeared.

One evening after sunset Fatima was relaxing at home when she heard the plaintive cry of a *boza* seller from the street below. She glanced across at Fulya who was watching a film on TV. 'It's unusual to hear a *boza* seller at this time of year, isn't it sis?'

Fulya listened to the man's persistent cry for a moment. 'Yes, it's getting a bit warm to drink *boza* but I'd quite like to have one now.'

'OK, I'll call him up,' Fatima said, opening the window and shouting, '*gel, gel, buraya, bozacı.*' She heard an answering cry and went to open her front door. The *boza* seller stood, a pole across his shoulders from which dangled two trays. He handed Fatima a glassful of the golden yellow liquid; his mouth, which was covered in a bushy moustache, twitching into a grin. Fatima stared hard at his unshaven face, his baggy Turkish trousers and his threadbare jacket. 'Can, can this be you?' she whispered. His answering nod caused her to fling the door open. He followed her inside and Fulya jumped up from the settee and gave him a hug, almost knocking over the glasses of fermented wheat drink.

The twins began to speak at once, firing questions at him until he held up his hands. 'Slow down, girls.'

'Oh, Can, *özür dileriz*. We are sorry, but we are so pleased to see you,' said Fatima.

'And I you.' Can had sunk down onto the sofa, his face drawn and tired.

'Please tell us how you come to be selling *boza* – when did you get out of prison?' Fulya asked.

'A few days ago. I bribed the guard and then I looked up an old friend who set me up as a *boza* seller. It's a good disguise but I can't live like this for long, the police will be looking for me. Anyway, enough of me. What have you two been up to?'

Fatima took a sip of her drink, noticing its faint alcoholic smell and sweet, slightly acidic taste. 'We've been trying to find places to belly dance, but it's not easy. Word has got out about the police raid and our involvement in it.'

'That's too bad, Fatima. What have you been doing for money?'

Fatima looked at Fulya and frowned. Her twin sat up straight and stared at Can. 'I went to the yacht and took some of Zeki Bey's cash. I hope you don't mind, Can.'

Can gave a deep sigh. 'As long as you haven't spent it all, Fulya. I need money to get out of here.'

'We've been very careful, haven't we, sis? Fulya said and Fatima nodded. 'There's still plenty left, plus the drugs.'

'That's all right then. I don't suppose you've got any cigarettes?'

'Sorry, Can. You know we don't smoke but I can go and buy you some,' Fatima said.

'No, that's OK. I should give up anyway.'

Fatima had been thinking hard. 'Would you like to stay here for tonight? Fulya can sleep with me and you can have the couch.'

'That's sweet of you, Fatima. I will if you don't mind but I'll leave in the morning. I'm going to go to the yacht and then disappear.'

'Disappear? What do you mean?' Fulya asked, a look of concern on her face.

'I mean I'll sail to another country.'

'Oh,' Fulya said, her voice cracking and her eyes filling with tears.

'Please don't cry, Fulya. I'll be fine. I'm used to escaping.' He looked from one twin to the other. Fatima sat dry-eyed, emotionless, while her sister dabbed at her eyes with a tissue.

'Let's go to bed now, Fulya. I'm sure everything will feel better in the morning,' Fatima assured her.

*

Fulya awoke first in the morning and lay listening to pigeons cooing outside the window. She thought about Can's sudden appearance and his imminent departure. She did not want him to go.

Fatima opened her eyes. '*Günaydın.* You're awake early, sis.'

'Yes, I know. I'm thinking about Can.'

'I was dreaming about him escaping from prison. You're sad that he's leaving, aren't you?'

'Yes, I am. I didn't realise how fond of him I've become. Would you let me go with him?'

'What do you mean? You want to leave on the yacht?'

Fulya noticed how upset Fatima was but nevertheless she continued. 'I don't want to leave you, my dear sister, but I think I love Can and I want to be with him.'

'Oh! But he loves me, not you.'

'I know that but I hope that in time he'll come to care for me.'

'Well, if that's how you feel I'll have to let you go. He might not want you with him though.'

'I know that. We'll just have to see,' Fulya said, getting out of bed.

Can was almost unrecognisable when he came to the breakfast table: his stubble was turning into a beard, his hair was unkempt and his eyes had dark shadows beneath them. The twins tried to cheer him up but he remained withdrawn, eating little food. Finally Fulya could stand it no longer. 'Please let me come with you, Can,' she blurted out, her eyes never leaving his.

He stared at her and shook his head but then said, 'If you really want to come, Fulya, I would like that but I'll have to get you a passport.'

Fulya restrained herself from leaping up and hugging him and focussed on asking him questions instead. 'Where are we going and how easy will it be to get me a passport?'

'I'm planning to sail along the Black Sea coast to Sochi in Russia and I should be able to get you a passport through my contacts. You never know, Natalia might even be there.'

'Natalia! Isn't she still in gaol?'

'I doubt it. Ladies like her manage to charm their way out of unpleasant situations. Anyway, she wasn't really involved in the drugs operation.' He gave a short laugh, wondering how his father was being treated behind bars. 'Anyway, do you have any photos?'

'No, of course not. I've never needed one,' Fulya said, her face glum.

'But I thought I did and I have some,' Fatima said. 'They're recent so they should be OK.'

'I'll go out and do it now and take the *boza* stuff back,' said Can, taking a photo from her. He tried to smile but his eyes were looking sadly into his darling's.

Once he'd gone the girls busied themselves with housework, trying not to worry about his possible capture. In the late afternoon he came, clutching a passport which Fulya took, full of excitement. 'We should get going, Fulya. Are you ready? We have to go by bus as I no longer have my car.'

'Yes, I have only one bag.' She turned to her twin, put her arms round her and squeezed her tight. 'I won't say goodbye, sis, just *au revoir*,' she whispered into Fatima's hair. Fatima managed to stem her tears until they had gone. Then she sank down on the sofa, buried her head in her hands and sobbed and sobbed.

*

A few days later Fatima went to look at the restaurant and was surprised to find it open. She went inside and looked around at empty tables, then she saw her boss emerge from the back room. 'Fatima! *Hoş geldin*,' he said, and kissed her on both cheeks.

'Mehmet Bey! It's good to see you. When did you reopen this place?'

'Let's go into the back room,' he said, looking pointedly at the waiter who was busy laying tables. He shut the door and continued. 'A couple of weeks ago and before you ask, let's say that I helped the police with their enquiries.'

'That's great but what if Serkan Bey also gets released?'

'There's no chance of that. I heard that he died in prison.'

'Oh! Do you know how that happened?'

'I don't but I can guess. Our police employ fairly brutal interrogation methods.'

'I see. And what about Zafer Bey?'

'He's probably still in jail, let's hope for a long time.'

'Yes, let's hope indeed.' Fatima looked inside her cupboard: all her costumes were still there.

'Have you found any other work?'

'No, I haven't. It's been difficult. I tried together with my twin sister but a lot of restaurant and bar owners round here had heard about the raid and didn't trust us.'

'That's too bad. You may return here if you like. There are less customers than before but it should pick up soon with tourists. Where is your twin now?'

Fatima told him about Can, Fulya and the yacht, trying not to get upset. 'That's quite a story, Fatima and I hope it has a happy ending.'

It was arranged that Fatima would start the following night and she hurried home, keen to phone Gemma and tell her the news. They had hardly seen each other while Fulya had been staying with her but now she hoped that this would change.

'That's wonderful news, Fatima,' Gemma said, adding, 'when can I see you, it's been ages.' They started making plans and Fatima was pleased to hear that her friend had finished with Hasan. 'I didn't trust him any more after the raid,' she admitted.

*

Gemma floated in the hot water. The stars were out, the air smelled of blossom and frogs were croaking ecstatically in the warm waters of the *Termal's* stream. They were alone in the pool and she glided over to Fatima and kissed her. 'Oh, Gemma. This is the most beautiful place I have ever been,' she said, returning the kiss. The hazel-eyed attendant appeared and circled the pool, arranging the loungers in neat rows. He greeted Gemma who replied politely. 'Do you know that guy?' Fatima asked.

'He was here when I came with Tina, that's all,' Gemma said, thinking *I don't need his massage now. I hope that I have everything I want right here.*

Ackowledgements

I would like to thank the Tyne and Esk Writers (Musselburgh group) and particularly Catherine Simpson, our writer in residence (2016-18), for their unfailing patience and constructive criticism. I would also like to thank my sister for her assistance with editing.

Printed in Great Britain
by Amazon